A Cape Mounted Rifleman

A Cape Mounted Rifleman

Four Years' Service in South Africa
During the Kaffir Wars
1877–1881

An Ex C. M. R.

LEONAUR

A Cape Mounted Rifleman: Four Years' Service in South Africa During the Kaffir Wars, 1877-1881
by An Ex C. M. R.

Originally published under the title
With the Cape Mounted Rifles: Four Years' Service in South Africa

Leonaur is an imprint of Oakpast Ltd

ISBN: 978-0-85706-318-2 (hardcover)
ISBN: 978-0-85706-317-5 (softcover)

http://www.leonaur.com

Publisher's Notes

Contents

CHAPTER 1

Introductory

I write with no view of presenting to the public a history of the wars with the native tribes in South Africa, which for the last four years have been raging in that distant and extensive colony, but to give the friends of the many and gallant men who are serving in the C. M. R. a general, plain, and straightforward idea of the life experienced in that popular corps, in which it has been my fortune to pass through many strange scenes and perilous adventures. With this single object only I desire to lay my small volume before the public, hoping that my narrative may be found interesting. The wisdom of English statesmen will be long and largely taxed to devise and carry out the means of pacifying and settling these vast territories and the swarming population with which they abound. To have been through these regions, and to have become familiar with the multitudinous tribes, the larger number astute, warlike, and intractable, presenting the dispositions common to all savage people, of treachery and distrust, is to have become saturated with convictions that none but wise, patient, comprehensive, and strictly just and impartial counsels can avail anything in prosecuting so great and important a work. Any vacillation, change of feeling, or the absence of a vigorous prosecution of the means which may be deemed best, would be worse than futile. We are dealing with a colossal question, and shall find no satisfactory solution of it except we are prepared to act like giants.

In the latter part of the year 1876 I returned from the west coast of Africa, my health being considerably impaired by that insalubrious climate. Having no immediate employment in England, and finding an idle life in London too dull for my liking, I turned my thoughts towards enlisting in the Frontier Armed and Mounted Police in the Cape colony, believing at the same time my health would be recruited by such a step. At the time to which I refer this corps was attracting much attention, and the agents of the colony were holding out considerable inducements to encourage men to join what was regarded as a popular force, in which promotion from the ranks was a condition and stipulation offering strong attraction to the recruit.

On paper, as presented to the confiding youngster, these inducements appeared well enough, but except on paper they had no real existence whatever, as I thoroughly discovered in a short time. The conditions entered into with those who joined were in one case and another broken in every particular. As this departure from the stipulated terms made with the men at starting is a subject to which, as I proceed, I shall have occasion somewhat fully to advert, I set out the agreement in full, that the reader may be the better able to follow and judge of the fairness and impartiality of my observations.

Articles of Agreement made and entered into this day of   187 , between A—— B—— or C—— D——, of 10, B—— Street, in the City of London, acting for and on behalf of the Government of the Colony of the Cape of Good Hope, or by

of

on his behalf, on behalf of the Government of the Colony of the Cape of Good Hope, of the one part, and now living at   of the other part.

The said   for the consideration hereinafter mentioned, hereby undertakes and agrees to proceed forthwith to the Colony of the Cape of Good Hope, in a Vessel to be indicated by A—— B—— or C—— D——, and that he will upon his arrival there report himself to the Government, and diligently and actively serve the said Government as a member of the Cape Frontier Armed and Mounted Police Force, upon the terms and conditions mentioned and contained in the Schedule hereto.

8

And the said Government hereby undertakes and agrees, by the said A—— B—— or C—— D——, to provide the said

with a free passage from   to the Colony aforesaid and to the Head Quarters of the said Force, with rations during the passage and until his arrival at such Head Quarters as aforesaid. And further to pay, or cause to be paid, to the said

                                             wages

at the rate specified in the Schedule hereto, and in all other respects to observe and perform all the conditions on their part mentioned and contained in the said Schedule hereto.

IN WITNESS whereof the said parties have hereunto set their hands at   the day and year aforesaid.

THE SCHEDULE ABOVE REFERRED TO.

1. The Frontier Armed and Mounted Police is a force maintained for General Service, either within or beyond the borders of the Colony of the Cape of Good Hope.

2. The age must not be under 18 years, nor above 30. The maximum height to be 6ft. 1in., the minimum 5ft. 4in. Weight not to exceed 160 lbs.

3. The period of service is three years from date of joining the Head Quarters of the force.

4. The wages commence at 4s. 6d. per diem from the day of arriving at Head Quarters, and are increased to 5s. upon the recruit being mounted and appointed to second class, and to 6s. on his obtaining the rank of a *first class* private. During the time any member of the Force shall be incapacitated for or absent from duty through illness, so much of his pay only shall be drawn as may be necessary to defray the cost of his maintenance and treatment and the keep of his horse. A return of undrawn pay under this rule will be rendered monthly by officers commanding troops to the Commandant, and by him to the Colonial Secretary.

5. A horse and an entire outfit is provided from the equipment fund, and a stoppage of £2 per month is made from

the pay until the cost thereof, which averages £40, is repaid. Upon the man's discharge, the horse, accoutrements, and outfit so provided, become his own property, and may be disposed of as he deems fit.

6. According to the Cape Act of Parliament the men are bound to supply themselves with rations and other necessaries; but to enable them to procure provisions with greater regularity and cheapness, arrangements are made by which men who desire it are enabled to draw rations daily, the cost of which is deducted from their pay.

7. The men are required to pay for the keep of their horses; but forage is provided as cheaply as possible by officers commanding troops. As the men are paid 5s. per diem as soon as mounted, there is no deduction for forage until they receive that sum.

8. Officers and non-commissioned officers of the force are, as a general rule, selected and appointed from its ranks.

9. Losses sustained by the force when on duty and occupied by encounters with the enemy, when duly certified by a Board, will be compensated according to the following scale:—

Horse £14 0 0
Saddle and Bridle 5 0 0

These prices to be the maximum.

10. Rewards will be given for extraordinary diligence or exertions, and compensation for length of service, or wounds, or severe injuries received in performance of duty.

11. The members of the force must conform to the rules and regulations established for the discipline and efficiency of the service.

Witness:

For the Government of the Colony of the Cape of Good Hope.

Having presented myself at the office of the agent, and having been cautiously and carefully examined by a doctor, I put my hand to the above agreement, and became bound "to serve the Cape Government for three years in the Frontier Armed and Mounted Police." The Cape Government at the same time became a party to the Agreement; but, as I shall show, treated it as waste-paper, according as the occasion suited them and those they had placed in authority. The enticing and encouraging terms of the engagement which caught the recruit remained unfulfilled, the promises were repeatedly and undisguisedly broken in defiance of law and the regulations professedly laid down, and in spite of the determined and repeated remonstrances of the unlucky wights they had entrapped into the service.

For brevity's sake for the future in my narrative I will call the force the F. A. M. P., that being the title by which the force was known in the colony, until subsequently it was converted into the C. M. R. (Cape Mounted Rifles).

On the 29th of March, 1877, in fulfilment of my agreement, I proceeded to Southampton, to embark on board the *Teuton* S. S. belonging to the Union Steam Ship Company. By way of introduction to the authorities of this ship, let me give a brief sketch of what the Union Company in this instance gave us as a comfortable and convenient passage to the Cape. The agreement with the colonial agent having stated that for the recruit a free passage with rations would be provided, that condition should honestly have been observed. Now, whether the fault lay with the Union S. S. Company or the agents for the colony, I am unable to say, but the fact remains: we, being twenty-two recruits in number, were all consigned to the same berth as were the steerage passengers. Never was greater disorder or discomfort experienced; the passage was a free one with a vengeance, as will be seen.

We were placed on a part of the deck abaft the second-class cabin, to be associated for the whole voyage with a low set of ruffians. From the day we left Southampton, until we arrived at Port Elizabeth, we never had any meal without a fight for it. A considerable number of navvies were proceeding by this ship to the Cape,—the roughest of the rough, as might be supposed,—and when a meal was due our time was chiefly occupied in defending ourselves from the attacks of these men in their eager search for food. The continual scrambling was both detestable and disgusting. Unfortunately we had a long and tedious passage to the Cape, twenty-eight days being consumed in the voyage.

The reader may possibly ask what else could be expected? If gentlemen elect to go out as private soldiers they must not be fastidious. As far as myself and two or three more were concerned, we cared little about the matter. Having served a long apprenticeship in various services, and in various climes and countries, and having encountered many hardships and privations under many trying circumstances, and several of my comrades having enjoyed similar experiences, we determined good-humouredly to make the best of it. Nevertheless, when a formal agreement is made to give a free passage with rations, as respectable Englishmen are not disposed to question the preparations made by an authorized agent, they do not anticipate that a "free passage with rations" implies consignment to piggery and discomfort of every kind, with a free fight for every morsel of food to be supplied.

It was a piteous sight—to see mere lads of sixteen and seventeen years of age doing battle with these strong, ravenous men for their daily food. But the scene, revolting as it was, was no more than a foretaste of what they were later on to experience. Several of my companions, like myself, were of gentle birth, but much younger and without any experience of the world; they had not long left school, and had come straight into this pandemonium from a well-ordered home. Larky as they were at first disposed to think it, such daily scrambles soon tired. Fancy what it was for such youngsters to have daily a fight for their food! Cricket and football did not come as a very appropriate preparation for such a state of things. The first tussle with the world could have seemed neither agreeable nor encouraging. Only English pluck carries men through such scenes. But the sight, could it have been witnessed by their friends, would not have been edifying or consoling, who no doubt were comforting themselves with a full recollection of the conditions so amply set forth in the agreement, believing they would be faithfully observed. Well, everything, whether bad or good, comes to an end, and the reflection I have always found abounding in consolation. In due time we reached the Cape. We were speedily conducted to a magistrate's office, and sworn in to serve in the F. A. M. Police, and obey all lawful commands," &c. So there was an end at last of dinner scrambling, navvy company, and all the rest of the steerage filth, which had been foisted on us.

After remaining three days at the Cape we sailed for Port Elizabeth and East London. At the latter place we were to disembark. At Cape Town, through the watchfulness and activity of the agent there, we had been joined by six additional recruits. These six men were, without exception, the most unmitigated ruffians it has ever been my luck to encounter: one was a regular down-easter Yankee, the most awful brute you can conceive; two were select Irishmen from Liverpool, precisely of the same social rank as the Yankee; the remaining three were Englishmen, but of a very bad stamp. The lot were runaway sailors, and had been enlisted at the Cape that the agent there might put into his pocket some few trifling fees for this addition to the force. I will undertake to say, that these six men would in a short time corrupt a whole regiment of well-disciplined soldiers, let alone such a force as at that time was the F. A. M. P. I shall have something more to say of these men as I proceed.

At Port Elizabeth one of our party gave us the slip, and it was a matter of regret subsequently to some others that they did not take themselves off in like manner. On arriving at East London we were put under the conduct of a sergeant of the F. A. M. P., who was dressed in a fancy costume of his own devising. We accompanied him to a wooden shed, to which he led the way, about a quarter of a mile out of the town. To each of us was then given a red blanket, with some biscuits and some tinned salmon. After this we were left for a time to our own devices.

In this shed the six men who had joined us at Cape Town, all without exception, got very drunk, and commenced fighting every one they could see. As I was with four others occupying a separate room in the shed, and being fully able to take care of ourselves, these ruffians deemed it better not to molest us; and as the rest of our comrades cleared out of the building, they were left in full possession. In a short time, drunk as they were, they went after the sergeant who had conducted us to the spot, and having found him, proceeded to beat him in the most cruel manner. After a while they were stopped and arrested and put in confinement for the night. Peace once more reigned in our lodging. On the next morning we were all taken by train to King William's Town, to the police barracks, and handed over to the sergeant in charge. He left us to take a shake down, which all of us were glad to do; and so terminated my start in the F. A. M. P.

Chapter 2

Arrival at the Cape

The police barracks at King William's Town stand a short distance outside the town. They are built in the form of a square, having within seven rooms, a guard-room, and a stable with accommodation for about eighty horses. In these seven rooms there is convenient space for no more than thirty men. But at the time of which I am writing there were sixty men at the station, and to these were added the twenty-seven men, the party with which I had joined the corps, making the place intolerably full. We could not occupy the station, and were therefore put into camp at the back of the barracks to receive our initiation into the mysteries of the force. I very soon discovered what these mysteries were. Conversation with some of the older men, who had been some time in the service, convinced me the orders and regulations were simplicity itself. These old stagers were naturally desirous of making the recruits as like themselves as they might be able, and with such intent used no reservation whatever in their description of the corps. Said one of them to me, in the simplest and most confiding manner, "Never do anything you can help doing." Another said, "If they make you begin at anything, do as little of it as you can." A third then chimed in with advice sufficiently definite and comprehensive, "Give," said he, "as much trouble as you can to the officers and non-coms, and they'll soon learn to let you alone, and you won't have a bad time of it." War had not yet broken out, and being a time of peace, the men had become lazy and indifferent. The time came when all this was changed.

I soon found that what these veterans had alleged was substantially true. The non-coms were too immoveable to trouble themselves to rouse the idle; but if they found you willing, they worked the willing horse to death; and if you gave them trouble, as the old fellows had said, they let you alone for peace sake, with much less trouble to themselves. This was the general state of things throughout the corps; but there was an exception. I must do the force the justice of stating that all the troops were not in the same unsatisfactory and disorganized condition. The Artillery troop especially was commanded by an experienced military officer, and the discipline in this troop was good. But of the nine other troops, including that at the depot, if there was anything approaching fair discipline in one or two, the remainder were very decidedly neglected and unsatisfactory.

Whilst on this subject, it may interest the reader to have a very short account of the origin of the F. A. M. P. The force was formed by the late Sir Walter Currie, and at the time it was organized consisted chiefly of farmers' sons and others thoroughly acquainted with the country. These men all spoke Kaffir and Dutch, and as policemen were not equalled. They did not pretend to be highly disciplined, and as a fact had nothing approaching military drill. They could come and go quickly from one point to another, could *spoor*[1] cattle, could trace thieves, and could all ride and shoot well, being thoroughly used to native manners and customs.

After a time the Cape Government commenced to recruit for this corps in England and elsewhere, and attempted to make the force semi-military. This they failed to accomplish. They spoiled the corps as a Police Force, and retaining the officers of the former body, precluded altogether the maintenance of military discipline, with which the officers were not acquainted. The officers were good enough and valuable as police officers, were, in fact, all that could be desired for the oversight and command of constabulary, but as soldiers they were valueless. They knew nothing of a soldier's duty or drill. They knew about as much as a soldier does of a ship. Still the Cape Government persisted..

---

1. To track.

They were bent on turning the Mounted Police into a cavalry regiment, made to order, without officers acquainted with the drill, or men who would submit to drill, or listen to reason. The result of this grave mistake was but too clearly discovered soon afterwards, in the early days of the Galeka war, when only by wholesale flight and narrow escapes did the police force get extricated. After the death of Sir Walter Currie Commandant Bowker was appointed. He tried to put things into a better shape, knowing a little what they ought to be like. For a time he persisted in his course, and the corps was gradually acquiring something like discipline. But being repeatedly snubbed by the Cape Government, he at last gave it up as impracticable, and the force soon relapsed into the old system of " do as you like," officers, non-commissioned officers, and men being utterly indifferent to all regular discipline and duty.

The men being more numerous than the officers, decidedly had the best of it. Such was the state of things when I joined the force as a private, keeping advancement fully in my eye. Three years later, when I left the force, things were totally different. A new government had come into office at the Cape, and had the good sense to put military men at the head of the force as the only direct and certain way of converting it into a military body. Police duties had been for years a thing of the past, and police officers should have been earlier as well as entirely suspended. Even at this time, in the few troops of the C. M. R. in which old police officers continue in command, great awkwardness is noticeable; whereas the troops commanded by military men are smart and look like soldiers. What advantage can there be in giving police officers the military rank of captains and majors when they are ignorant of the simplest cavalry movement, or how to effect it? They refused to learn the drill and evolutions, and were continually setting up antagonistic opinions, and encouraging adverse feelings with those of the troops of the C. M. R. who were well disciplined.

The day they are superseded and pensioned off will be a good day for the colony, and the C. M. Rifles will hail it with acclamations.

Among the class of men from which these effete and impracticable officers were taken, it was not to be expected that any large amount of education would be found. But at least care should have been taken to ascertain, prior to their promotion, that they could pen an order in English, which could be understood; as a rule, it was quite the contrary.

The reader, I fear, will begin to tire of hearing so much respecting this race of inefficient officers which, I am glad to report, is fast becoming extinct; so I relinquish the subject, to return again to the first days we passed in the barracks at King William's Town.

Our usual routine did not present much variety of life. We were drilled every morning on foot for an hour, after which we went to breakfast. Breakfast over, a stable fatigue was the order—to clean up the square and the stables. After this the men were free to do anything they liked till five o'clock p.m. At this time a roll-call was made. The men fell in and answered to their names, and were dismissed. This was repeated at nine o'clock p.m. Day after day this course was continued, and became in a little while most tiresome and monotonous. Happily it lasted no longer than a fortnight for us recruits. Our Cape Town friends, the six ruffians to whom I have particularly referred, had been let off lightly enough, with a fine of two shillings and sixpence, and with the simple caution not to repeat their misconduct. I mention these facts to show the sort of discipline observed at that time in the F.A.M.P.

Pay-day, however, came round, and was too much for these fellows, four of whom again got very drunk; and as beating sergeants seemed to be their specialty, they tried it again. This time, I rejoice to say, they caught a tartar, and were placed in custody in the guard-room for the night. Three days afterwards, being brought before a magistrate, they were sentenced to six months' imprisonment with hard labour, and to be dismissed the force. For this we were all heartily thankful. Of the remaining two, one shortly afterwards ran away, and as he was certainly not worth the trouble of catching, nothing was done. The last died after a brief interval—the result of his excesses. Thus all six disappeared from the service, as they will from these pages. But I regret to state that there remained in the force too many men of the same kidney, whose acts of blackguardism and irregularity nothing could exceed. Enough of these ruffians. I have simply-described them as I found them, the bad with the good, that my record may supply the reader with an accurate knowledge of the force.

I must not omit to mention, that all the stations occupied by the police were erected, such as they then were, by the men themselves, and at their own expense. Except arms and ammunition, everything was at the cost of the men; and as their equipments had to pass through the hands of a quarter-master holding the rank of Inspector before they reached the troops, it will easily be understood that he had very nice pickings out of us. He soon became a rich man, this quarter-master, owning several farms well stocked with cattle and whatever he thought necessary. On the other hand, in consequence of a system so disgraceful, the men, as may be supposed, drew very little pay at the end of each month, and naturally became very dissatisfied.

One of the great and very serious disadvantages of the irregularities which were permitted was, that no fixed time was ordered for meals: this threw everything out of gear, till complete disorder prevailed. All the cooking, cleaning, and internal economy of the camp had to be performed by the men, and it continually happened that they were called away in the middle of their meals, and sometimes when they had just sat down, to go on some fatigue or some other duty. If any tried another hour for breakfast, say next morning, the chance was they would be again disturbed and called away. In fact, whenever it suited the whim of the sergeant in charge, he would call the men out. All this was simply on a par with everything else in the camp; order, regularity, discipline, there were none, nor any attempt of the kind. All was disarranged and in confusion. Should a man come late on parade his being reported was by no means certain. If the non-commissioned officer happened to be afraid of the man, nothing would be said about it, and the offender would get off scot-free. Should the offender, however, by chance be put into the guard-room, the sergeant who put him there would have to look after him, or the guard would probably let him go, and the prisoner would be sure to slip out at the first opportunity. Should his offence at last come to the officer's ears some trivial excuse would be advanced, and the officer would be satisfied with telling the man "not to do it again." This was not quite the way to correct parade irregularities; so that, what with the bullying of the non-coms, and the easygoing or indifference of the officer in command, so little impression was made on the man that absence from parade became common.

Things in the artillery troop, I am glad to say, were very different. Captain Robinson, the officer in command of this troop, made it his regular practice to be firm about everything. He inspected every batch of recruits arriving from King William's Town, and took, from these as many as he desired for his own troop. I had heard a good deal about him and his men from the old hands, and had resolved to join his detachment of the force if possible. I was inexpressibly glad when the report reached me that he was coming one morning to inspect us, and select men if likely to suit him. We had all fallen in. He walked down the line, and I well remember how anxious I felt, hoping he might choose me. I happened to be in the middle of the line. He stopped at the next man to me, and addressed him thus:

"Can you drive?"

"No," was the reply.

"Well, then, can you ride?"

"Like the very divil himself," shouted Paddy.

Black grew the brow of the interrogator, and then followed a good-natured smile, as he said, "It is not customary to make those sort of observations to your commanding officers."

" I beg your pardon, sorr," said Paddy at once; "I forgot meself." So the affair ended. The captain then turned to me with the same question, " Can you drive?"

"Yes."

"What?"

"Anything and everything."

I had been used to the whip all my life, and could handle a mail, phaeton, tandem, or coach and four, no matter what; so I answered confidently, and was accepted. To make a long story short, the captain took down six names, my own included, and that night, to my intense joy, I received orders to start for Komgha the next morning.

CHAPTER 3

Life in the Force

The six men selected for the artillery troop, as I have related in the preceding chapter, were all of the party who came out with me in the *Teuton,* so that five of my fellow-travellers were still with me. The remainder were despatched to the depot at Fort Murray. Respecting Fort Murray and the system maintained there I shall have more to say later on. But at present it may be well to state that at the time to which I am now referring it was *supposed* to be a musketry instruction depot for the whole force. It was very suitable for this purpose in all respects, the station being commodious, with good barracks and stables. In the Cape Colonies *supposition* goes a long way, and resembles charity, which covers a multitude of sins. This is particularly the case with regard to the military service of the colony. Fort Murray never got beyond the supposition that it was a place of great advantage. In theory it was a depot; practically it was nothing, as will be shown further on.

The next morning our party was mounted. Except carbines and revolvers, our uniforms and all our equipments were served out.

Let me first describe the uniform as then appointed. The reader will be familiar with the expensive and becoming dress of an outside porter at any of our principal railways. Now, imagine this corduroy dress to be dipped in log-wood dye till it becomes as stiff as a piece of thick card-board, and there is the old uniform of the F. A. M. P. in 1877. Add to the corduroy dress a cap with a small peak, leggings of leather to go over the trousers, and the costume is complete. For all these clothes the men had to pay; and for the articles I have mentioned, costing in the colony about £2, they were charged £3 10s. The officials, it may be supposed, imposed this extra cost for the dye. This clothing when dry was so hot that you longed to throw it off; when wet, it was so heavy the men could hardly bear so great a weight.

In time these clothes certainly became softer, but they were badly made and of bad material.

Of the rest of the equipments the saddles were good and cheap, costing about £6. The bridles and headstalls, though heavy, were excellent: in fact, all articles in leather were of the best material and workmanship, and no fault could be found in the price. Whatever the cost reached, it must not be forgotten, the men had to pay, and the sum was stopped by instalments taken from their wages till the whole was discharged.

Now, as to the horses. By selling horses indirectly to the recruits, a temptation which the system suggested and encouraged, the officers made more money than the amount of their pay. There were some few whose honour would not permit them to follow this questionable course. The rule of the force was this: as the trooper had to pay for his horse, a town dealer would bring a lot up to the station, and after the required number had been selected by the officer, each man was ordered to pick one of these for himself. He was allowed two trials, but if he did not fancy one of the animals, the third time he was compelled to take one, whether he liked the horse or not. What was called a Board was then assembled, consisting of one non-commissioned officer and two privates, and, not without the suspicion of a *douceur* from the dealer, they proceeded to determine the price of the horse. This decision was final.

For the sum of £20 or £25 the trooper became possessed of his horse; generally the animal was in poor condition, without too much flesh on his bones. If he got in his bargain two sound legs out of the four, he was supposed not to have done badly. The age also was most probably what is known in the force as "Cape age"—anything between six and sixteen.

This horse dealing, if I may be pardoned for using well-known descriptive terms, was one of the biggest swindles out.

In nine cases out of ten the horse was worth no more than ten or fifteen pounds, and in many instances would be dear at that price; but it must be remembered that the dealer had so many expenses that he was compelled to "stick it on;" and this pernicious system was winked at and prevailed, with gross injustice to the men. One dealer whom I knew well, and with whom I had afterwards a great many transactions, never brought up horses for selection for a less price than £25 a piece, whether big or little, any size, shape, or condition: he knew what the price was and stuck to it. I suppose he was right: it was his living.

Knowing all about horses myself, I asked and obtained leave to buy one elsewhere. I soon found an excellent horse suitable for my purpose, and well up to my weight, and purchased him for £25. He carried me well for eighteen months, and I sold him at the end of the time for £45.

Some of my comrades, having poor eyes for a horse, did not do so well; and when we were all in the saddle we made together but a sorry lot, as I looked at the mounted party when we were preparing to start for Komgha.

The reader may now picture in his mind's eye a F. A. M. Policeman fully equipped. A well-made man of middle size, on horseback: a huge blanket, waterproof coat, and a large valise strapped on in front of the saddle, and reaching together nearly to his chin, and over which the rider can just see. Behind, a most capacious pair of saddle-bags, covering the entire flanks of the horse, a tin pot or two suspended to the straps of the saddle-bags, with an axe and any fancy article which the trooper may deem necessary, stuck in promiscuously wherever these can be arranged. I have seen a pair of large and heavy boots appended to the head collar, and a frying-pan to the crupper. The horse seldom likes this last arrangement at first, and no doubt feels very much like the dog with the tin kettle tied to his tail: but he soon gets used to it.

One horse in the artillery troop when we were on patrol used regularly to have strapped to the saddle-girth a small kettle, which hung underneath him, and apparently he was quite indifferent to it. This was of course done by way of a joke, and was omitted if an officer was of the party. A more sagacious horse than this to which I am now referring was seldom met with. He was named Rufus, a bright chestnut, and was a wonder in many ways: he was about twelve years old, and had been in the force from the age of three years. He knew all the bugle calls as well as the men, and all the roads within a hundred miles. His owner was in his way as peculiar as his horse, and the two went through some strange adventures together when they left the troop some twelve months from this time. On this occasion the poor horse was loaded by his master in all possible parts, all his worldly possessions hanging from the good-tempered beast in every direction.

But to return to Komgha. From King William's Town, on this occasion, we had to escort a wagon fully loaded with ammunition to the station, and proceeded the next morning with a sergeant of Artillery in charge of us. Three days were occupied on this duty, though the distance was no more than forty miles. We reached Komgha about eight in the evening of the third day. A strange accident befell me this very evening. I went to fetch some water hard by, and took particular notice, as I went, of the path which led me to a small stream. I was unable to find my way back to the barracks, and as it was as dark as pitch, simple as had been my decent to the burn, I was two long hours before I found my way back, though the distance did not exceed five hundred yards.

Our new comrades, who had heard we were coming, received us with much kindness. They had a good meal ready for us, consisting of meat and hot coffee. Throughout the force at this time there was a strong feeling of good-fellowship. All the members of the troop I was in, made, in a quiet, unostentatious way, main sacrifices for their comrades; and the kindnesses which were exchanged are not likely soon to be forgotten.

Komgha is a small village about forty miles northeast of King William's Town. The village consists of a few stores and a couple of hotels, as they are called in the country. These hotels, as might be supposed, were much frequented by the F. A. M. P.; the landlords of both rapidly made their fortunes, and retired after a few years. They were good, honest fellows, and did the members of our troop many a good turn.

Half a mile from the village stood the artillery barracks, a brick building of three sides of a square. On one side were the stables, on the other side were the rooms. In this troop we mustered but forty-five men, so that the accommodation was ample, and the troops soon found themselves in comfortable quarters. We six new recruits had allotted to us a room apart from the rest, and we soon settled ourselves into shape.

As this troop became my home during three years, I shall be forgiven if I describe matters in detail. Let me commence with the officers. Our captain was an officer in the Royal Artillery, and had served with Her Majesty's forces in the Crimean war, an excellent fellow, beloved and respected by all the men, and as excellent a soldier. Of our other two officers, one was an Irishman, not a bad sort; the remaining one a Scotchman, and no good at all. The former was a peppery, hot-headed, devil-may-care kind of man, but right and just in all essentials. The latter, in a word, was a sneak. I have no desire to abuse him behind his back, and under the cover of anonymity; but as he experienced a fair share of abuse to his face, if he should read this I feel sure he won't mind it. The Irishman, notwithstanding his faults of hasty temper, we all liked. He used to stir us up smartly every now and then, but he was never ill-natured or a bully. The other man was unreliable, he was all vinegar one day, and all sugar the next.

A body of men such as we were wanted ruling with a firm hand. No one sought favours, or wanted more than his deserts. I must do Captain Robinson the justice of stating that he kept the troop in order. He seldom had occasion to resort to punishments, and when he did they were never excessive.

In the Artillery troop I found life very different to what it was when I was stationed with the troop at King William's Town. At Komgha everything went on according to strict military routine. The life was consequently full of regularity and comfort. Each knew what his duty was, and it was his own fault if he neglected it and got into trouble. Our officers here set their faces like a flint against any horse-dealing in the troop, such as I have described. The first result of this was that the men were all well mounted, having the value in the cattle of the money they had paid. Being well mounted they could be kept in a high state of drill. They were neat and clean in their persons, and dressed as well as their strange habiliments permitted. If these prevented them from presenting the appearance of soldiers, they at least looked like a well-ordered body of men. The arms we then handled were a 9-pounder Woolwich pattern, and three 7-pounders R. M. L. The expounder was mounted on a field-carriage, and the three 7-pounders were on mountain gun-carriages. All of us were regularly drilled to both sorts of work, and were thoroughly efficient. In fact, the troop was in good order, and I believe without exception was the only troop in the corps in this satisfactory condition.

We had gun-drill four days in the week. Saturday was devoted to a clean up; and on Monday we invariably had a saddle parade, when all our arms and equipments were carefully inspected by the officer.

After drill till 5 p.m. we had literally nothing to do except cleaning up for the next day, which, with an occasional game at football, filled up the afternoon. The men in the interval could do as they pleased.

This life was not, in the ordinary acceptation of the word, hard; or indeed unpleasant, after you had settled down to it; the monotony only was at times trying. That was soon to end, as war was near at hand.

At 5 p.m. we fell in by bugle. The horses were brought in, cleaned and fed in the square, inspected by the officers, and then tied up for the night. At 8.30 we again fell in, answered to our names, to see if any were absent, and after this no one was permitted to leave the quarters without special order, which was only given once a month. In this we found the principal hardship. Young men don't care to go to bed at so early an hour, and there was nothing to do in the barracks.

At 6 a.m. punctually we had all again "fallen in," and woe betide the man who was late or absent. The non-commissioned officers did their duty, and insisted on the men doing theirs.

This is really the way to make a troop comfortable. The senior sergeant of the troop had been six years in the force, and was rather strict at first with recruits. He had a difficult post to fill, but he did it in the best way he could. Eventually I became very friendly with him. There were three other sergeants in the troop, and four corporals. These were all of a good sort, kept themselves very much apart from the men, and were encouraged to do so by the officers; they were fairly educated, and as long as the men did their work they did not bother them. But the force now contains a very different class of non-commissioned officers— steady young men, of good stamp, disposed to make the force their home, and stick to their profession. Eventually these will become officers; some, in fact, had obtained a commission before I left South Africa.

CHAPTER 4

Rumours of War

I will now put before the reader extracts from official despatches which have been published respecting the actual condition and discipline of the whole F. A. M. P. force.

Up to the time of which I am writing, July, 1877, it must be remembered that this was the only colonial force, and that native affairs were beginning to assume a very serious aspect. The farmers were daily complaining of the loss of their cattle by thefts committed by the natives. With a part of No. 3. troop, which, like ourselves, was stationed at Komgha, we were on constant patrol in search of the thieves. Sometimes we were successful in capturing them, but oftener not. The natives by night drove the cattle right away from the district, and so escaped detection. From personal knowledge, and from my frequent conversation with many of the frontier farmers of standing, I know they were at this time in a constant state of anxiety and alarm as to the future behaviour of the Kaffirs.

The statesmen in Cape Town, all-wise as some deemed them to be, expected to govern a country by some extraordinary arrangement, some twelve hundred miles from their reach, and of which they knew little or nothing. They were themselves in perfect safety from any Kaffir attack; and as their own life and property were secure, they ridiculed the fears and statements of these men on the frontier, whose whole life had been passed among these savages, and who, from experience, knew the ways and customs of the tribes. Many of these farmers were intimate with several of the chiefs, and in some few instances had formed a personal friendship with them. Difference of opinion with the ministers of the colony, seated in their bureaux at Cape Town, produced no effect but to excite ridicule. One of these ministers, speaking at a public dinner, gave expression to views totally at variance with those of the farmers who were on the spot. I quote from a Cape newspaper. "I am sorry," said he, "that these men on the frontier, who have taken up positions there and received land for nothing at all, in consideration of their being called upon to defend the country, should be the first to be scared and to run away at the moment of danger." I must remark on the part of these farmers, that whether this statesman was sorry or not, none of the farmers cared one jot! As a matter of fact, they did not run away, neither were they scared; and not until the Kaffirs in large bodies were howling around their homesteads, did they go into *laager* at Komgha. Everything the farmers predicted took place. They were able, from their experience and knowledge of the tribes, to foresee what would occur; and they were following a course perfectly constitutional in laying their misgivings before the ministers of state. They knew too, full well, the condition and extent of the only force that could turn out to help them: a mere handful of men against thousands on thousands, who would band together whenever war was begun.

After a few more remarks of no importance this speaker went on to say: "I am glad to think that not only his Excellency the Governor of the colony, but also the general and the Military, all understand one another perfectly, and that if anything occurs we shall stand together, and let the enemy see it, and they will regret the day that they entered into conflict with us. I do not consider that there is any occasion for alarm."

It may be he did not. He was in Cape Town, and perfectly safe. The government had failed to acquaint themselves with the facts. It is not possible that the speaker could have known the threatening attitude of the natives, or have considered the state of the force at this time. Whether the Kaffirs or ourselves regret the day, as this minister suggested, he can now answer for himself. No man living can say when the hostility of these tribes shall cease. The Galekas to this day do not consider themselves beaten, and will, without doubt, rise again on the very first opportunity. Their chief Kreli has never been captured.[1] I have seen him twice since the termination of the war; and though he admitted he was driven out of his country, he declared to me he could again draw round him a great body of his old fighting men if he could see an opportunity; and I quite believe he will.

After I left the C. M. R. I had several Galeka servants. These made no secret of it that they would be obliged to leave if he sent for them; and I have heard the same from many people of great experience on the frontier. The important question seems to be, how the colony is to maintain adequate forces at different centres on the frontier, so as to be prepared for any outbreak of the natives when it may occur.

I must return now to make some further remarks on the F. A. M. Police, which may enable the reader to understand well and accurately the position of affairs in the colony in respect of the means of protection which were supplied.

The force consisted nominally of one thousand men. I have already mentioned that *supposition* goes a long way in estimating military arrangements in the colony, and it went very far certainly in this instance. Whether the returns were falsified or not, I am unable to say, but the force more probably never exceeded eight hundred men. The troops of this force, altogether inadequate in numbers to the duties assigned to it and the services expected of it, were distributed as follows:

Artillery—in which I served,—Komgha

No. 1	Queenstown
No. 2	Kokstadt
No. 3	Komgha and Grey Town
No. 4	Palmeitfontein, and Kei River
No. 5	King William's Town and district
No. 6	Transkei
No. 7	Peddie

---

1. Since writing these pages Kreli has surrendered himself to the government, and has been located within a few miles of where his "Great Place" originally was; and here, safely protected by the Exeter Hall party, will train up the young men of his tribe to make war upon the white men, whenever they may be strong enough as a tribe, or can combine with other tribes for the same purpose.

No. 8	Kenhardt
No. 9	Ealing's Post
Depot	Fort Murray

The arrangements and organization of the force were as follows:

A commandant in charge of and commanding the whole force, with his head-quarters and staff at King William's Town.

His staff consisted of pay-master, sergeant-major, three sergeants, two corporals, and three privates. All these were employed in office work.

In each troop there was an Inspector and two sub-inspectors. All with one exception had risen from the ranks, and this one exception had exchanged from the civil service. There was a sergeant-major to each troop, and the allowed number of sergeants were divided amongst the whole force.

The rank and file of the force, so far as *personnel* was concerned, was excellent. It was the custom in the colony to say that the men were broken-down clerks, and young racketty men who had run through their money, and others who were unable to find employment at home. The allegation was far from correct; a mixture of men was to be expected. There were a few clerks who might be called broken-down, but I know that the force comprised a large number of good, able men, and if scapegraces there were, they were far out-numbered by the higher grade. Nevertheless, I have known men who have thoughtlessly run a muck, pull up and make excellent soldiers; and the fault of the force was not traceable to any deficiency in the calibre of the men, but to the utter absence of true discipline and proper organization.

I have already referred to this neglected condition of the force in some particulars, but I shall be excused if I revert to the subject in a few additional remarks. Where was really the fault in all this? Why was the force improperly organized, ill-disciplined, badly officered? The answer is, that the officers, as a rule, were not gentlemen; and a mixed body of men as we were were not long in making this discovery. Thus it happened that the men were systematically neglected. In our troop the difference was manifest because we were privileged to have a gentleman over us. In the other troops the officers lounged about, swearing at the men, were frequently drunk, and were very imperfectly educated. They were totally ignorant of the simplest evolution; they were too lazy and pig-headed to take the trouble to learn it. A few notable exceptions there happily were, but my description is a fair one of the officers of the F. A. M. P. at that time, and of the consequences of such supervision and command. For a patrol everything a man possessed had to be squeezed into his saddle-bags or haversack, and strapped somewhere on him or his horse; and thus of course with six days' provisions he could not be expected to present a very attractive appearance to the observer. There was no provision for the sick, or for transport of ammunition or provisions, no commissariat beyond the saddle-bags to which I have alluded; and when the war did eventually break out, the sick, wretched men were for days literally starved. Beds in barracks there were none, tents for the field there were none, until the authorities, no doubt hearing of the complaints, introduced a patrol tent, six feet long and three feet high, to be shared by the two men who were charged to carry it.

I cannot do better in this place than quote the report of an officer who was on General Cunynghame's staff, and who was sent by the general to inspect the depot. After the usual official introductions of the report, he says:

Although due notice had been given of this inspection, when Captain Parr arrived on the parade ground five minutes after the hour for which the muster had been ordered, he found that some of the men had still to be sent for, and others shouted for. Of one portion of the detachment very few were provided with uniform, and many of them wore excessively uncleanly and disreputable clothes, and some of them were personally very dirty and unwholesome in appearance.

The report goes on to state, that as far as the inspecting officer could discover, no instruction had been given in the use of their arms, or, in fact, anything else.

There were only ten horses, one of which was a two-year-old. Some of the men could neither speak nor understand English.

This officer then went on to Fort Murray, the depot station. After a vivid description of the filth of the whole place, he winds up by saying:

I found the barrack-room strewed with debris of all kinds—old mattresses, rags, bits of board, and branches of trees tied together to serve as beds.

Such was the condition of the depot which was supposed to supply the force. Can it be wondered that men became disgusted with such a state of things? Could there be any discipline or *esprit de corps* under such circumstances? Desertions were of course frequent. In some cases the men got clean away with horse and all equipments, and every one helped them to escape as much as possible. If a man fell sick, whether by accident or disease, all his pay was stopped, and only enough given him to feed his horse and himself. This was a great hardship, and most unjust; the very hardiest constitutions would at times give way under such work as we had to perform; but as a rule, the men stood it better than the troops of the Imperial forces, though the latter had every attention, tents, food, &c, whatever was needed. But when the Galeka and Gaika wars were over the F. A. M. P. men gave way; their health, it was found, had been undermined by rough work and neglect, and they died in numbers at King William's Town of dysentery and fever contracted in the field.

On the breaking out of the Galeka war the Cape government contrived to collect about five hundred men, including the Artillery Troop, to hold Ibeka. These men were fairly mounted and equipped, but imperfectly drilled and disciplined. They, however, got into better form during the war, and as most of the fighting was in the bush, the individual intelligence of the men enabled them to make many good stands against the Kaffirs, who were at least double or treble their number. The officers, of course, took all the credit of the fighting, though they had little or nothing to do with it. The men had nearly always to dispose themselves as their own judgment seemed best. Some of the officers, in fact, as is well known, proved themselves arrant cowards, only full of wind and bluster, and deserted their troops when brought face to face with the enemy.

I have before said there were exceptions to be found among these men, but the general run of them behaved as I have stated.

It was a knowledge of this which made several commanding officers in the field afraid of employing the F. A. M. P. Of the fighting qualities of the men they were in no way in doubt, and knew they were all "eager for the fray;" but they also knew perfectly well that their officers were not to be trusted, that they would lose all control over their men, and that irretrievable confusion would result. If the Kaffirs rallied, as they frequently did, such a state of things would simply mean wholesale slaughter for the unlucky men, through mere want of discipline.

In the force there were plenty of men who well understood military duties and routine. These had served in H. M. service, and would have made excellent officers and non-coms; but they were kept back and out of sight, that the ignorance might not be exposed of the officers already in the corps.

It will easily be understood how all these matters made many of the men thoroughly dissatisfied with the force. We had all been led to believe that we should join a thoroughly well-equipped and disciplined body; but everything was misrepresented from first to last — pay, conditions, state of corps — in fact, everything.

As far as pay is concerned, the men would have received more as privates in any line regiment, though we were led in England to believe, as expressed in the agreement, that we should receive five shillings a day on joining. So we did, it will be alleged; but there were such a multitude of stoppages and drawbacks out of the prescribed pay, that at the end of the month, instead of drawing the agreed £7, our pay, as a rule, seldom exceeded twenty or thirty shillings. Comfort we had none. Encouragement was on the same scale. We had joined for three years, and were forced to make the best of it.

Such was the state of the force to which the Cape government was looking to defend the frontier against hordes of native warriors. That it utterly broke down till the force was re-formed and re-organized was not surprising. After the Galeka and Gaika wars we were made the nucleus of the present gallant and well-ordered force, the Cape Mounted Rifles.

CHAPTER 5

The Transkei

To return to Komgha. About the beginning of August some new gun-carriages arrived for us from King William's Town. With these we at once became very busy, as they required fitting. Charge of the government horses was committed to me, and I was promoted to the rank of corporal at the end of about three months—my first step in the force. My duties were very simple. They consisted in breaking-in the gun horses, looking after the drivers, and driving one gun myself. The guns were three 7-pounders; they were driven from the limber box, and each drawn by four horses.

A fortnight soon passed in this way, and during this time rumours were frequent of trouble arising in the Transkei.

We took the precaution of having more constant drills, exercising frequently the gun horses, filling also the limbers with loaded shell, and keeping the men served with extra ammunition. These proceedings, with a mounted patrol every night reconnoitring all the country round and adjoining Komgha, told us pretty plainly that something was up. In a short time half of us were under orders to sleep dressed every night, and the officers remained during the night in the barracks—a thing they had never done before.

Some time after this No. 7 troop arrived from Peddie, and was encamped at Komgha. At this time the frontier farmers were frequently coming in and holding interviews with the several officers in command of the three troops massed at Komgha. Still for the present nothing was distinctly told to the men, and we all continued anxious. With the exception that we were constantly out all night watching the drifts or fords of the Kei, everything went on in the ordinary course.

At last, one night, the sergeant-major came into my room and said, " Get up at once;" at the same time telling me to have ready No. 3 gun, and that a detachment was going to Ibeka. "You will have yourself," he added, " to drive the gun there, and then return. A man will lead your horse. You will be wanted to start at daylight, and it is now two o'clock."

Accordingly I jumped up at once, saw the horses fed and got ready for "spanning in." At daylight we started, with the gun and a detachment of twelve men, an officer of artillery, and fifty men with an officer of No. 3 troop.

No. 3, though not in a state of military discipline, was in a very fair state of order as a police troop.

The road from Komgha to the Kei River is full of interest, and in many parts very picturesque. It passes frequently through beautiful avenues of white thorn trees (Mimosa), varying from fifteen to twenty feet high, but broad and expanding, giving a pleasing effect to the scene. The spine of this tree produces a bad and obstinate fester both on man and horse; but singularly enough, mules and goats eat the leaves and prickles apparently without inconvenience.

Seven miles out of Komgha, on this road, is a large farm known as Pullen's farm, belonging to a man of that name. We found him as mean, inhospitable, and disagreeable a fellow as it is possible to conceive. The frontier farmers, as a rule, on the contrary, are hospitable and agreeable to all without exception, and I have received many kindnesses from them at different times. This man was quite an exception; he was a sworn enemy to all mounted policemen. My comrades reciprocated his hatred. It was bad policy on his part; it would have been far more to his interest to have cultivated a friendship with them, for in these wilds men were not slow at retaliation. Refusing to sell the men poultry, of which he had plenty and to spare, and for which the men would willingly have paid a fair price, he was despoiled of it in a wholesale manner whenever a troop was passing there. I cannot defend what was nothing short of robbery, but I always felt the fellow brought those losses on himself by his dog-in-the-manger temper.

On those farms where police troops were stationed during the war the proprietors never lost an egg, and their poultry, as well as all their possessions, were of course respected. The men were always prepared to buy; but in a case such as I have mentioned, where the owner would not sell, helping themselves was the only means left to the men to obtain food. Who can blame them?

From Pullen's farm the road winds circuitously down a very precipitous hill to the River Kei, or Grand Kei, as it is here called. This road passes immediately under a hill known as Maunder's Kop. When Sir Philip Maitland was encamped here this hill was the scene of a dreadful tragedy. A party of his officers rode up to the top to obtain a view of the surrounding country. The Kaffirs observed them as they were ascending the hill, and climbing up by a steep and rugged path, which none but a Kaffir, a goat, or a monkey could do, made an immediate attack on these officers. A terrible fight ensued. The Kaffirs were in overwhelming numbers, and the result was the entire destruction of the Englishmen, some of whom were *assegaied*, and others captured and hurled over the precipice, not one escaping to tell the tale.

The Great Kei was then the boundary between British Kaffraria and Kaffirland. The tribes in this land consist of Galekas, Tambokies, Pondos, Bomvanas, Pondomise, and Fingoes. There were, and now are, a number of sub-tribes; but those I have mentioned may be taken simply as constituting the principal tribes occupying Kaffirland. The chiefs of these tribes were as follows: of the Galekas, Kreli; the Tambokies, Gangeliswe; the Bomvanas, Moni; the Pondos, Umquiqela and Umquiliso; the Pondomise, Umthohonolo and Umditchwa.

The Fingoes had no chief as understood by the other tribes, but they all more or less recognized as their head a man called Veldtman, a Fingoe, who had received a semi-English education, and who with some few Fingoes did excellent service during the wars which followed soon after the time of which I am writing.

All these tribes which I have mentioned, with the exception of some of the Fingoes, lived in the must primitive and barbarous manner. Amongst them witchcraft, with all the gross and revolting cruelties attached to that system, is universally practised. Clothing they have little or none; nor did they want any. A blanket was the almost universal dress. A continual feeling of jealousy existed between the adjoining tribes, making them always ready for war. Especially was this the case with the younger men. They entertain an intense hatred for white men. On this account great trouble and perplexity are occasioned for the authorities. Except for trade, the Kaffirs voluntarily hold no manner of intercourse with the white population. A chronic state of disturbance from some cause or other, with white and with black, is to be regarded as their natural condition. I formed this opinion of them from the experience I acquired while living in the midst of these tribes.

The Galekas especially are a brave and warlike race, and had been panting for a long time for battle. The Tambokies, on the contrary, are a most cowardly people, and are without a single good trait. The Pondos are capable of some discipline and order; but as to courage, are little better than the Tambokies. The Bomvanas are also cowardly, but still are warlike. The Pondomise perhaps fight better than the other tribes; they are well mounted, and are not afraid to charge again and again, but are difficult to rally when repulsed.

The Fingoes, who are everywhere friendly with us, can fight at times fairly well, if led by white men. Their defect is, and it is a serious one, they are liable to panic, and therefore cannot be relied on.

All the tribes fight with such arms as they possess, chiefly *assegais*. They in no case give quarter. They thrust and stab, not always killing; but they invariably, whether the enemy they have overpowered be dead or living, rip up the stomach of the fallen foe.

A party in South Africa maintain, that we should interfere as little as possible with these tribes; that the only course we should adopt is that suggested by the "Kilkenny Cats." We should encourage the tribes, they say, to make war on each other, and they would soon eat one another up.

Of the wisdom of such a feeling I do not myself pretend to judge. I know that were it pursued the complete destruction of these tribes would follow. Anyone who is well acquainted with their ways and dispositions will not doubt for a moment that such would be the ultimate result.

All over the country the Cape government are placing magistrates of ability at various centres, and the natives are encouraged to lay their complaints before them; but in Kaffirland they have not proved a success for many reasons. Some of the gentlemen who might prove able magistrates in civilized districts are unsuitable for the duties required of them. Some temporize with the natives; others treat them with undue severity. Some are always on the side of the natives, so offending the frontier farmers who may have lodged complaints; many are the reverse of this, and know not where to draw the line.

The missionaries of all denominations often impede, as well as impair, the action of the government. Having, in many cases, influence and power over the chiefs in whose country they may be resident, they fear to lose the ascendancy they have acquired. With these qualities it becomes impossible for them to render any assistance to the government, and they are encouraged to thwart measures which would promote the general welfare. I have known a great many; some of them were good, amiable, and pious men. But if I entertain a very high opinion of a few, I regret I must acknowledge that my opinion of the rest is not flattering.

Many men who have failed in business at home or in the colony, sometimes as traders in the very district where they are located, have turned missionaries from no conscientious motive, but as a means of getting a living. They all become rich; they live in good houses; they have everything they want. Having regard to this state of things, I have often thought of speeches I had heard in England referring to the poor missionaries in Africa, spending their lives among the heathen, and a lot more nonsense of the same kind. If they who talk thus only knew how exceedingly comfortable and well-off these missionaries are, I have no doubt they would gladly change places with them.

As a counterpoise to many of these men who are very disreputable, there are a few who really do good work, and who do it from thoroughly conscientious motives. These have given up good positions at home to come and labour among the Kaffirs and other poor benighted tribes. Need has not driven them to the exercise of their profession. Some of them have good private incomes, and spend liberally in maintaining their mission stations, and in assisting the members of their various congregations. Too much honour cannot be given to these good men; they labour without any to praise or encourage them, and are content to have the approval of a good conscience. If all the missionaries in Africa were like these exceptional few, the condition of things in the colony would be very different.

I know of a strong case in point: one of these missionaries, a bankrupt trader, who failed some six years ago for a very large amount; he has now a splendid house, he is the owner of between three and four thousand sheep; in addition he possesses about five hundred head of fat cattle, and three wagons.

Now this man had to leave the country for a time to escape being prosecuted for some dishonest transaction, seeking refuge in Kaffirland. He there started "the missionary business," and has become possessed of what I have stated. How he must have prayed and swindled, and preached and swindled the unfortunate Kaffirs amongst whom he pitched his tent, it is quite needless to remark. The Kaffirs in his district, as many of them have told me, would be glad enough to get rid of him; but a magistrate has been appointed to this district, and he thus gets protection. In consideration of the good he has done as a missionary, pardon has been accorded him in respect of the criminal offence he had committed. The good he has done to the Kaffirs is not so apparent as that he has done to himself, and were enquiry instituted, it would be found there was more harm than good done, as far as the natives are concerned.

Another missionary anecdote and I will leave the subject. A man I well knew as a missionary on my first arrival in South Africa, I met again in Pondoland, shortly before my return home, that is to say, after an interval of about four years. He was trading at this time with two wagon-loads of goods. He had blankets, red clay, beads, and other things for barter with the natives. I asked him at once how it was he had abandoned his mission station. He told me, without reserve, that he had made a good bit of money, and that, as he had never altogether taken to mission work, he had returned to trade. So he was first trader, then bankrupt, after that missionary while it suited him, and then he took to trade again. Writing as a layman, I cannot but reflect on the impression such a state of things created in my own mind. Should this man again fail in his trade speculation, no doubt he will return to missionary enterprise. I commend to liberal donors to missionary societies these few facts out of some of my experience in Africa, and shall perhaps induce the charitably disposed to discontinue indiscriminate benefactions towards the poor missionaries labouring among the heathen in foreign parts; I might add, to the improvement of their banking accounts, and the benefit of the colony.

CHAPTER 6

The Campaign Begins

The Kei is a river running between high hills, having its source in the Stormberg Mountains. It varies very much in volume. There are several fordable drifts in it, which are passable in the dry season; but when the river is *down,* as it is termed when in flood, these fords are most dangerous, and at times impassable. Before the present fine bridge was erected, and which was completed in 1879, many lives were annually lost. This bridge crosses about twelve miles from Komgha, and is built of iron supported by twenty-four iron columns filled with concrete. The river was *up,* that is, not in flood, when we arrived at one of the fords on our way to Ibeka, and we had little difficulty in getting through. I was subsequently four days waiting to get over with a cart and six mules; and when I made the attempt, at the urgent request of some officers I was taking to the colony, we were nearly drowned; the cart and ourselves being swept some distance down the river. Luckily the mules pulled through somehow by themselves, and beyond a severe ducking, we were none of us much the worse.

But to return to the narrative of our journey. The road from the river to Toleni, the place at which we were to stop for the night, is very precipitous, narrow, and bad. Used as I had always been to driving, it took me all my knowledge and experience to get up and down some of these hills; but the horses pulled well together, and we at length reached Toleni. The last four miles of the road were simply cut out of the side of a hill; with no more than room for the wheels, and with very sharp turns in it. If the slightest mistake or slip had been made, we should have gone down many feet, guns, horses, everybody, and everything. We reached the top, however, all right, and were not sorry.

At the present time there is a very good road, avoiding the hills altogether, and this might as easily have been made first as last. Toleni is a trading station, consisting of a house, shop, and outbuildings, and was then kept by a surly, ill-conditioned, half-bred Dutchman, who, when a police troop was subsequently stationed there, refused to serve them with anything at all. As this was the only place within twenty miles where the common necessaries of life could be obtained, the police were compelled to help themselves.

For miles round the place not a tree was visible, except at a missionary station belonging to one of the reverend gentlemen I have before mentioned; and here everything was of course per-fection except himself. At Toleni we outspanned for the night, and cooked our suppers. Having fed our horses with *mealies* ob-tained at the Kaffir store, we rolled ourselves in our blankets, and with our saddles for pillows, slept the sleep of the weary and the good. In the police force the horses were always "rung" at night. The way in which this feat is accomplished is very simple. The *reim*, a piece of raw hide about six feet long, is made fast to the head collar of the horse on your right, doubled, and so on until the horses are all fastened together. The two horses at either end are then attached to each other, thus bringing the formation into a circle. Two sentries are then posted, one inside, one out-side the circle. By this method the horses are all kept perfectly quiet. In the morning at the first dawn of day they are let loose to feed on the *veldt*. The sentries are relieved every four hours.

As I had gone through a good deal of campaigning at various times, I improvised a small tent, which I carried on the gun limber during the time I was driving. Many a drenching was I saved by my foresight in this respect, and as I had no difficulty in finding a chum to go halves with me in the tent, we used to take it in turns to cook and manage. On the whole I did not find my new life irksome, and, considering all things, I was not uncomfortable.

The next morning we started for Butterworth. The road is

very uninteresting: the country is nearly all the way perfectly flat and unwatered. Butterworth is a mission station, situated on a river bearing that name, and containing a couple of stores, a missionary residence, and the usual buildings. A neat little church also stands here, and the appearance of the whole place is pretty and attractive. Two miles from this the recognized head of the Fingoes lives, Veldtman, to whom I have already alluded. All this country, from the Kei upwards, is populated by Fingoes. These Fingoes (Fingoes in Kaffir language signifies dogs, and is the strongest term of reproach which is used) were originally slaves to the Galekas and other powerful tribes. By the intervention of the English government they were set free, and have gradually become rich and numerous. Great jealousy exists between the Fingoes and the tribes who formerly owned them as slaves. Veldtman lives in a house built in European fashion; he has a church close to his house, and a number of families live on or about his location. A native Kaffir clergyman resides here, and a very respectable fife-and-drum band belongs to the station. In the district are several magistrates. The whole of the surrounding country looked flourishing, and the people seemed well-to-do.

The country is of the same flat and uninteresting description, with very few trees; these are chiefly thorns, and stunted in their growth. We stopped here for the night. Next morning a messenger came from Komgha with an order that we were to remain at Butterworth for the present; so we formed a camp close to the banks of the river, and made ourselves as comfortable as we could. The next day No. 7 troop arrived and encamped by our side. There were now some 170 police at Butterworth. The Fingoes came for a talk to us daily, bringing eggs and milk for sale. From what they told us, it seemed to be pretty certain a storm was brewing. An order came that I was to remain with the gun until another driver was sent. This I found inconvenient, having expected, on my safe arrival with the gun, to have been sent back to Komgha; and in this expectation, I had hardly brought a change of clothes. Nevertheless, orders were orders, and had to be obeyed; so I made the best of it, borrowing some garments, and settling down to this new state of things.

The Fingoes continued to impress on us the certainty of the Galekas attacking them at no distant time. They informed us they were all selling cattle, and buying guns and ammunition. The butchers also assured us that the Galekas were constantly enquiring for ox-tails and skins, which they use as charms in war. At the time we did not attach much importance to this information; but as I learned by experience afterwards, when Kaffirs sell their cattle, and enquire for tails and skins, they mean mischief. In addition to this, the Galekas were beginning to be very insolent and overbearing towards the storekeepers; they did not hesitate boastingly to tell them that they cared nothing about buying much, as in a short time they would be able to take what they wanted. It was known that they were "doctoring" for war; and though all the farmers and others on the frontier communicated to the authorities that these sayings and preparations were indications of war with the white population, the government refused to believe it. They supposed it to indicate little more than a trivial squabble with the Fingoes, and that nothing of a serious nature would come of it. At any rate, some 170 or 180 mounted police were all the force they moved up to Butterworth.

Shortly after this, on the 26th August, the whole of the Artillery, with No. 6, No. 9, and part of the depot troops, were marched to Toleni. I was recalled from the Butterworth detachment, a fresh driver being sent up in my place, and I reached Komgha the day before we were to leave again for Toleni.

As I had driven so lately up the Kei hills, I was not embarrassed by this second drive so much, though I was extremely thankful when it was finished.

At Toleni a camp was formed, and then commenced a continuous round of drilling and of putting into shape all the troops which were there. We drilled incessantly, going through the same movements again and again. All, I think, became pretty sick of it at the time; but I soon afterwards saw how necessary all this training was, and in how much greater peril we should have been placed if things had been allowed to go on in the old way. During the time we were encamped here our commissariat was well supplied. Each troop had obtained a wagon-load of groceries, and meat was to be had in plenty. This, however, did not continue.

In the beginning of September parts of No. 6 and No. 9 troops were moved up to Butterworth. Matters were daily becoming more serious in every direction; the Kaffirs were going through all manner of performances with the witch doctors. In one instance two of the chiefs consulted their doctors, and these ignorant and superstitious wretches actually skinned two oxen alive, one black, the other white: as the white ox lived the longest, they concluded for the time there would be no war. What measures should be taken with people who believe in and practise such dismal and cruel rites?

During the second week in September Sir Bartle Frere and Mr. Merriman, the premier, appeared on the scene. They proceeded to Butterworth, with the intention of having, if it could be effected, an interview with Kreli, the chief of the Galekas. The old chief made all sorts of excuses, and would not visit the governor, sending one of his sons and several of his petty chiefs, but resolutely refusing to come himself. Sir Bartle and the premier returned to Toleni. On his return, Sir Bartle became very indignant when he discovered the Police had to live in small patrol tents. He at once ordered bell tents to be supplied to the whole force, and wagons to be hired to carry them. We thought things were looking up. It was a fortunate thing for the whole force that these bell tents were supplied, for without them the loss of life in the police force would have been very great. The rainy-season was coming on, which, with the cold nights, would have made great havoc amongst us.

Sir Bartle Frere returned to King William's Town, and on the 22nd of September, 1877, the entire available police force was ordered to Ibeka. The force assembled there on the 18th of that month consisted as follows:

Artillery	3 guns, 3 officers, 45 men
No 3 Troop	3 officers, 60 men
No 6 Troop	1 officer, 25 men
No 7 Troop	3 officers, 120 men

No 9 Troop was left at Toleni, and a part of No. 6 was left at

Pullen's Farm, to keep communication open. No. 1 troop joined us at Ibeka two days later: so the total of the force now brought together consisted of 13 officers and 295 non-commissioned officers and men.

This number included 3 officers and 65 men of No 1 troop. A camp was now formed, earthworks thrown up, and all due preparations made for what we knew must inevitably take place.

These works occupied us until the 24th, when Nos. 3, 6, and 7 troops were ordered, with a detachment of Artillery and one gun, to be ready for patrol.

On the 25th part of No. 5 troop, consisting of 1 officer and 40 men, arrived, They were also ordered out; but as they had just come off a march, the proposed patrol was postponed for one day. On the 26th, at nine o'clock in the morning, the above troops left for Idutywa. Little did we think when we saw our comrades march out of Ibeka cheering and in the best of spirits, that some of them would bite the dust before sunset. As they were on the point of starting, our new Commandant, Mr. Charles Griffiths, arrived. Our old Commandant's health had failed, and he was superseded by Mr. C. Griffiths. We knew nothing about Mr. Griffiths, and he knew less about us. He was an old police officer, but had been during many years the British resident in Basutoland, for which he was much more fitted than for his new appointment. He was never liked in the force, though he was a good deal better than some of those who succeeded him.

As the day wore on, we both saw and heard firing a few miles off. There were only the Artillery and a few of the men left in camp with two guns. The whole force there comprised 43 men. Natives (Fingoes) came in with the most alarming reports, one declaring all the police had been slaughtered, another that only a few were left alive, but all agreeing that our men were utterly and irretrievably beaten. We were kept under arms all night, lying down by the guns. If the Kaffirs had only then advanced in numbers, as they did six days later, they would have taken guns, slaughter-cattle,[1] ammunition, and everything else; but luckily they did not, or the writer would probably

---

1. All cattle intended for the butcher are called in the colony "slaughter-cattle."

have not been alive to tell his tale. I was not in this fight which took place about two miles from a hill called in Kaffir Guadana, and by the English Mount Woodhouse. The following is the official report of Inspector Chalmers, the commanding officer of the force engaged:

Lusisi Camp
October 28th, 1877
To the Commandant
F. A. M. Police
Sir,
In accordance with your instructions, I have the honour to report that, on the 26th *ultmo.*, while returning to Idutywa reserve, from the Ibeka camp, I was apprised of the fact that the Galekas had attacked the Fingoes on the government reserve near the Guadana. On receiving this information I continued my march along the main road, and when about two miles from the Umpuluse, opposite the Guadana, I observed the Galekas had crossed in numbers and attacked the Fingoes, and that an engagement was taking place between the two tribes. In obedience to orders received in the event of a battle, I proceeded to the scene of action in support of the Fingoes. Before taking any prominent part I sent back to the Umpuluse to acquaint Mr. Ayliff, who was there in command of a large Fingoe contingent, that the Galeka army had crossed into British territory. On the arrival of this gentleman with about 1000 Fingoes, I halted the gun and the men under my command; Mr. Ayliff with his Fingoes marching to the top of the Guadana Hill. In order to avoid surprise I sent Sub-Inspector Hamilton to Mr. Ayliff to receive a report of the position of the Galekas. This officer returned with a request from Ayliff that I should march on with the gun and men, which I did. On arrival there I found the Galeka army in three divisions at the foot of the hill. On our appearance the enemy made a move towards us; I immediately gave the order to the officer in command of the artillery (Sub-

Inspector Cochrane) to open fire with the 7-pounder, which he did.

After the 10th round, the gun became disabled, and on being reported to me I gave the order, 'The gun will retire under Mr. Cochrane and the escort.' This was immediately carried out, and the gun, under Sub-Inspector Cochrane and A. Maclean, with 25 men as gun escort, retired accordingly. Before entering into action my men were extended in skirmishing order, on the brow of the hill, the horses having been left out of sight, in hand, and in charge of the usual number of men. The Fingoes, under Mr. Ayliff, were placed on the left flank, between the gun and the Guadana forest, so as to command the bush. My men were placed on the right of the gun. When the Galekas came within rifle range I ordered the police to commence firing, and continuous independent firing was kept up for nearly two hours, which checked the enemy until the gun retired. When the Fingoes saw this they made a general retreat, running in among our horses and causing great confusion.

Finding that we were deserted by the Fingoes, and that by remaining on the ground any longer, the lives of the whole European police would be sacrificed, I ordered the men to retire. The confusion by the Fingoes rushing about in all directions caused several of our horses to break loose, and through this unfortunate circumstance one officer and six men fell victims to the enemy. The remainder of the men retired in order, and the gun was taken safely to the Idutywa. The firing from the 7-pounder was most effective, and so was also that of the Sniders. The estimated loss on the Galeka side was at least 200 besides wounded. I may say that the Fingoes, when asked why they retreated so soon, replied, that they had been watching the gun, and when they saw it move they thought it was time to leave the battle-field. I cannot attach any blame to our men in the engagement; they stood their ground until the very last, fired steadily; and were it not for the gun breaking down,

I have no hesitation in asserting that the result would have been different. Finding the gun and men were safe, I proceeded to the Ibeka camp in company with Inspector J. Maclean and Sub-Inspector Hamilton, where I personally reported the engagement to you, and returned to the Idutywa reserve on the morning of the 27th September.

The Galeka army must have numbered about 5000. Our force consisted of 180 men and about 1500 Fingoes. I have, &c.

G. B. Chalmers
Inspector commanding No. 3 troop, F. A. M. P.

Such was the battle of Guadana. It was fought under adverse circumstances, and in a nasty bit of country. The Fingoes fought badly, as they always do if they are not commanded by white leaders. They never stood, but retreated, firing, from the very first. Mr. Chalmers' account is substantially correct. I heard the same version from some men engaged, as well as from the Fingoes. The men who were killed, with the exception of Mr. Van Hohenan, lost their lives through Fingoes taking their horses; but there is no doubt that the last part of the fight was a desperate flight from the Galeka troops, whatever anyone may say to the contrary. I don't say the police ran away, because they retired in good order, until the Fingoes rushed in amongst them; but after that it was decided flight. Mr. Van Hohenan behaved bravely; he tried to take a man named Evans, who had been badly wounded, on his horse, and both he and Evans were shot down in their attempt to get away.

Some few days after, when, with a strong party, we went out to recover the bodies, we found all our poor comrades in a dreadful state. Evans had 17 *assegai* wounds in him; one man was scalped; Van Hohenan had his feet cut off; and all had their stomachs ripped open; all were stripped of their clothes. Not one of the party that saw this fearful sight but swore a fearful vengeance if ever we got hold of any of the niggers.

In the quiet of an English home I can look back with sorrow to the sights I have seen during my four years in South Africa; but I can hardly be expected to regret the part I took with my comrades in avenging the deaths of our friends at the battle of Guadana.

CHAPTER 7

Commencement of the War

As far as dates are concerned, I must now trust chiefly to memory, owing to my notes and other papers relating to the war having been burnt in my house at the beginning of the Pondomise rebellion.

Ibeka in Fingoland is distant from Butterworth seven miles; the road to it is very bad, large boulders of stone, and deep ruts, which make it very difficult to drive over. Constant care is necessary to avoid accident. The only building at Ibeka is a place belonging to Mr. John Barnett, since dead, consisting of a house, store, shop, and stable; the whole being surrounded by a wall built of earth and a ditch. The place was about 250 yards square. On our first arrival there we found a pretty garden, and several fine blue gum trees, which could be seen for miles. Mr. Barnett was a Kaffir trader on a large scale, and had resided several years at Ibeka. After the battle of Guadana he sent all his family away, and his house and premises were taken possession of by the police, the house being converted into quarters for the Commandant and Staff, the store into a hospital, and the shop into a magazine. We were now daily employed digging rifle trenches and making sand-bag bastions for our three guns at three different corners. Outlying and inlying pickets were posted every night, and every precaution taken to prevent a surprise.

It would be difficult for the reader to imagine the change that had come over the general discipline of the force. Everything was now done with order and regularity, and there is no reason why the same state of things should not have existed in time of peace. The duties required of the men became very heavy. Outlying and inlying pickets, of which I have spoken, and mounted patrols kept every one fully employed.

We were ordered to sleep in our clothes, our ammunition belts on us. The men were beginning to get sick of this sort of thing and wishing that the niggers would attack us if they meant to do so. A few days later our desires in this respect were fully gratified.

A party of Galekas about 500 strong, all of them mounted, rode up within a few hundred yards of the boundary with a white flag and an interpreter. We found that Sidgow, one of Kreli's sons, was in command of the party. He said he wanted to see the white men's chief. Advancing some hundred yards in front of his party, accompanied by a few of his men, he waited for Captain Robinson, who at once rode out with only two men, to ask him what he wanted. Sidgow replied that he had been sent by his father to say he was sorry the white policemen had been killed; that they only desired to fight the Fingoes, who had been stealing their cattle. He added he was very fond of the police, and did not want to fight them; he was sure they must be very hungry, and that, to show his good feeling for them, he was sending some oxen for them to kill for meat. Would the white chief take his policemen away, and let him pitch into the Fingoes? If he declined this, though it was greatly against his wish, he would have to cross the boundary in a day or two that he might thrash the Fingoes. Captain Robinson asked him what induced him to bring so many men with him. Sidgow replied, without reserve, that they were going to take a short ride into Fingoland, to see where the Fingoes were.

In the mean time our three guns had been run up close to this party and loaded with case-shot. Captain Robinson, addressing Sidgow, said, "Do you see these three guns? They are all loaded with case-shot. There are sixty-three bullets in each of those guns." He then added: "Go home like a good boy, Sidgow, and tell your dear Papa, that if he tries to cross the boundary he will be stopped, as you will be if you try that little move forward, in your kind enquiries after the Fingoes. If you, or any of you, attempt to cross, we shall fire on you, and the blood must be on your own heads. Take my advice, go home to your family, and tell them what you have heard; what I have told you is the word of the government."

Sidgow went back, and after a short palaver with his party, rode slowly off the way they had come.

In the afternoon of the day on which this occurred, a party of our men, twenty-five in all, went out for the purpose of trying to recover the bodies of the men killed at Guadana, which lies about fourteen miles east of Ibeka. When we were within four miles of the battle-field, we sent out some Fingoe scouts with a few police. We found the Galekas in force to the number of 3000 men, manifestly waiting for us. It would have been madness with a mere handful of men, to have attempted anything at that time; so we returned to Ibeka and reported what we had seen. Shortly after, this body of the enemy was seen marching towards Kreli's "great place," and several other groups were observed making for the same quarter. The conclusion we drew from this was, that Kreli was concentrating his forces for some mischief or other. The Cape government was now beginning to be alarmed; volunteers were being called out, and preparations were being made, but still on a small scale, for defending the frontier towns. A good round of abuse was discharged at the police everywhere throughout the colony, because they said we had run away from the enemy instead of stopping to be killed.

Some of these boastful critics I had an opportunity afterwards of observing, two years later, at the first attack on Morosi's Mountain. When danger appeared they did not decline to hide themselves in holes or behind stones.

Even at this critical conjuncture some of the ministry refused to believe there would be war. Everything was charged to the fault of the police and their officers. It was maintained that if the Galekas were only let alone and not interfered with, they would soon settle down and be at peace. The idea of a Kaffir war was thought and pronounced to be ridiculous.

Before two days had transpired ministers considerably altered their minds.

It was on a Friday morning. Early in the day large bodies of the enemy were seen continually marching towards Kreli's Kraal, which was distant from Ibeka about seven miles. We had our vedettes and scouts out all the day; but beyond finding that the enemy were collecting in large numbers, and exchanging a few shots with them, nothing of any importance occurred.

As we are now on the eve of the battle of Ibeka, I will give a brief description of the ground round about us, as on the following day it was to be the scene of a desperate and prolonged fight. The conflict between a few white men and many thousands of savages thirsting for their blood and plunder is better imagined than described. I have already mentioned the house and the sod wall surrounding the buildings at Ibeka.

To the east the ground gradually ascends, forming at the top a stony and elongated ridge, which slopes down towards the Xoxa River on the south. Towards Butterworth, which lies to the north-west, the ground is flat, with occasional boulders of various stones. Towards the north the ground is also flat for the distance of about a mile. It then slopes gradually down to the Butterworth River. In the front of the house, and facing the south, the ground falls directly by a gentle slope for at least a mile and a-half. This declivity is intersected by a small stream, which separates it from the stony hill I have already mentioned.

The ground is far more favourable to an attacking force than to those assailed, as affording a great amount of cover. Except at a long distance, the guns were only available on the south side; the low ground intervening, as I have said, supplied a most effective shelter to the attacking party. As a place for defence, therefore, Ibeka was not good. As far as the actual position was concerned, it was very defective; but it was the only place we could utilize, in the short time permitted us. Immediately in front of the house is the boundary between Fingoland and Galekaland. This boundary is denoted by a small footpath, with here and there an occasional cairn of stones.

In spite of the threatening attitude of the Galekas, a good many of the police had been sent away to hold other points of vantage, and on this Saturday morning there were only 120 men at Ibeka. This body of men, with 2000 Fingoes under Sub-Inspector Allan Maclean and Veldtman, together with half-a-dozen Europeans from the neighbouring trading-stations, constituted our entire defending force against Kreli's army.

Commandant Griffiths was of course in command, and we still had with us our three 7-pounders, and plenty of ammunition to supply them.

The accompanying map shows the positions of the attacking and defending forces at the moment of the attack.

At daylight we had received information of great importance from spies and scouts. The former told us that Kreli in person intended to attack Ibeka, the latter that the enemy were forming into columns of squares, that being their favourite mode of advance.

About eight o'clock we saw them on a hill, immediately south of us, in their usual formation, as intimated. Their numbers were estimated to be between 7000 and 8000. They halted about a mile and a half from us. Of this we took advantage to have breakfast, and to make a few more preparations for defence. The horses, which had been kept grazing close to what I shall now call the fort, were at once brought in, saddled, bridled, and tied up to a picket rope stretched between the trees in the garden. Shells and case-shot were brought out and placed in proximity to the guns; ammunition boxes were opened and placed all round the walls, and men told off to keep up the supplies. Barrels of water had been filled, and these were now set in convenient positions all round the enclosure.

When this was all done we went to our places, lighted our pipes, and waited the events which were to come. Most of us took our coats off to be freer for what I think we all felt would be a hard struggle. From one of three prisoners we captured after the fight, we learnt that Kreli was there in person, though he did not approach the front. His son Sigow commanded. Kreli's orders were to "destroy all the Fingoes, and on your way drive those troublesome policemen away. I don't like the sight of their tents; it disturbs me. You can breakfast at Ibeka, have dinner at Butterworth, and you will be then well on your way for the Komgha and the colony, where you will be joined by your friends," meaning the Gaikas. His orders were excellent, no doubt; but they did not exactly come off according to his expectation. A good many of his men slept round about Ibeka that night. They slept the sleep of death.

About half-past nine o'clock the enemy were reinforced by 2000 mounted men, who, after a brief halt, commenced creeping up to the stony ridge I have mentioned, and which is indicated on the extreme right in the map. The reader is to consider this ridge as our left, and the sloping ground on the south as our front. The whole of Kreli's army then commenced an advance. We lost sight of the columns for a time in the intervening hollows, the mounted men stealing up under cover of the ridge to our left. At this time the whole of Kreli's forces were no more than about 1700 yards distant.

The enemy, on approaching within about 1200 yards, threw out skirmishers, who began firing as they neared the boundary. This move was resisted by some 500 Fingoes under Veldtman, who despatched them to meet the enemy. On our extreme right Allan Maclean, with the remainder of the Fingoes, supported them, the police being thrown out in skirmishing order round the immediate front and left. When the mounted men of the enemy appeared over the ridge we fired at them with two shells; both, however, went over their heads. Two rocket tubes were then brought into action, and did great execution, frightening the horses, and causing many of them to bolt. We then commenced to fire our three 7-pounders, and the action became general along the whole line. Shell after shell was plumped right into the middle of the square columns, causing great slaughter. When the columns were broken after a little hard firing, the enemy extended themselves in skirmishing order, and again and again charged right up to us within 50 yards of the guns. Our fire, however, was too much for them, and they frequently had to retire to take rest; still at intervals coming on again and again, but with no better success.

Their mounted men were thus thoroughly broken up and dispersed by the rockets and shells.

At last, after several plucky charges, they collected together about five o'clock for a final effort. On and on they came, one scrambling, yelling mass, but only to be mowed down by our shell and rockets. Right up to the guns they came, and we poured shell, case rockets, and snider bullets into them with determined precision and effect, till at last they wavered. Down swept the Fingoes, with Allan Maclean leading them, and some 50 men of the police, led by his brother, Inspector John Maclean, cheering as they charged the enemy, and pouring in a heavy fire. As this section of our force advanced the Galekas turned and fled, leaving their guns, blankets, and everything behind them, as they ran for dear life, hotly pursued by the very men they had reckoned on easily beating.

The 7-pounders continued firing until the enemy was out of range. Till then we had no time to look about us. The fight had lasted from ten in the morning till five in the afternoon, and it was rapidly getting dark. Wonderful to relate, we had not one man killed, and only four or five wounded, and these wounds all were scratches. The Fingoes lost about forty men killed and eleven wounded.

The killed always predominate in native warfare. As the natives never spare the wounded, it is quite a chance if any such get away. How our men escaped is a marvel. Barnett's house was literally peppered with shot. The secret is, the enemy must, as all Kaffirs do, in their flurry have fired too high. Several horses were hit inside the fort. As the evening advanced, three Galeka prisoners were brought in, who told us that the whole army had suffered severely. We heard afterwards that more than a thousand were killed and wounded. These were nearly all removed by their friends during the night, in accordance with their custom. Some months afterwards we came across the place where they had buried their dead.

A heavy rain came on in the evening after the battle, and we could light no fires. So we had no coffee, food, or anything else, and the younger hands were beginning to feel knocked up, while the older ones were not much better.

We continued under arms all night, with our heads and the

muzzles of our guns pointing over the wall. A miserable night it was, raining hard, and bitterly cold.

At daylight the rain cleared off, and we saw that the Galekas had contrived to return very nearly to the positions they had taken on the previous day. We observed them creeping up again to the ridge, evidently with the intention, if possible, of turning our left flank. The Fingoes were at once ordered out and despatched up to the ridge. As the Galekas came within range of us they opened fire and retired. We also opened fire upon them with our three 7-pounders, at a range of 2400 yards, causing the enemy considerable astonishment; nevertheless, they continued to come on. For some time we fired, and they never got very close to us.

About ten o'clock in the morning a heavy fog came on, and continued till noon, when it cleared off, and left a bright day. When we looked, to our astonishment not a Galeka was to be seen near us. But we soon discovered the enemy at a distance of ten miles away, the fires of their camps showing where their armies had halted.

This was their first and last attack on Ibeka. The Galekas talk about it to this day, and have been unable to explain to themselves how such execution should have been dealt out from shell and rocket. They had never heard of or seen big guns before, and they were simply dumbfounded by the effect of a shell, and its possibility of bursting amongst them at 1000 yards with such deadly effect. Had they known the strength which numbers confer they could have walked over us. They fought well and pluckily, I must say. The way they repeatedly charged I shall never forget. They came with a determined rush, and if numbers only could have availed, they would have proved irresistible.

We now felt sure the Galekas would not again attack Ibeka, and they never did. We improved the walls, and made the fort much stronger, but this was labour In vain, for we never needed them more.

The whole colony, which had before lavished so much abuse on the F. A. M. P., now became loud in our praises, some of the papers writing the most fulsome articles respecting our gallantry and ability.

The government ordered us free rations, and seemed to think we were worth looking after.

As long as we remained at Ibeka we were in clover.

But the time was near when we were to be days and days without food, subsisting on Indian corn, or anything we could obtain. We were now preparing to make an attack on Kreli's "Great Place," which we were told was the next task to be set us. In the mean time certain events were taking place in the colony, to which I must devote a separate chapter.

Chapter 8

After the Battle of Ibeka

The government, after the battle of Ibeka, began to think that something was likely to come of these continual disturbances, as they were pleased to call them. The Gaikas, a large tribe of whom Sandilli was the chief, a drunken, dissolute old man, were at this time beginning to be troublesome, and No. 5 Troop was sent back to King William's Town.

General Sir Arthur Conynghame, the Lieutenant-Governor and Commander-in-Chief of the forces in South Africa, now assumed the chief command. He made his head-quarters in King William's Town, and placed Commandant Griffiths in authority over the Kei.

Detachments of H. M. 24th Regiment were sent to Komgha, Pullen's Farm, and Impetu. Large numbers of volunteers also, and some mounted burghers, were sent up to Ibeka, together with arms, ammunition, and provisions of all sorts. These mounted volunteers and burghers were well horsed and equipped, and were personally good men; but they were not in the slightest degree in any state of discipline. They did not indeed profess to be; they came up on the chance of capturing as many cattle as they could get hold of, in the belief that what they captured would be divided amongst them.

The great drawbacks to these corps were, that they could go home whenever they liked, if they were not, or did not consider themselves, properly treated. Some of these corps did after a while return home, but the greater part remained, and went through the entire campaign, and served manfully and honestly, long after there was any chance of cattle-lifting. Great credit, I think, is due to these men. Many of them were in business in a large way, and some of them were in good situations; and as a matter of interest from a commercial point of view, it certainly did not pay them to serve at five shillings a day, and to put up with all the hardships and inconveniences in the camp, to which the major part of them were certainly not accustomed. When all were collected, I suppose about 3000 men were mustered, including the mounted police. This force, with 5000 Fingoes organized under white officers, constituted our army. With this array Commandant Griffiths had to sweep Kreli's country, the natives of which amounted to about 18,000 or 20,000 men. I will now turn to notice the commissariat department.

I have already stated that there was no organization for the commissariat; but though the general, as it is now well known, pressed the Cape government at the proper time to allow him to commit this service to the charge of the officers of the Imperial commissariat, the colonial authorities refused to do so. They made every possible objection, chiefly on the ground of expense. The fact of the matter was, they bad brought on a war which might have been avoided, if they had listened to the frontier farmers instead of yielding to the opinion of the wiseacres of Cape Town; and now they had plunged the country into a war by their want of discretion, they begrudged the food and supplies to the men who were to fight their battles. As usual they were wrong, and were to find out their mistake, but at our expense.

The proper administration of the Imperial commissariat was always certain. The service never failed in any single instance to bring forward the necessary supplies: in respect of the question of expense, the colonial commissariat, when it was established, was far more costly, and was always uncertain.

On several occasions the police were for days without food of any kind. If we had not obtained *mealies* from the Fingoes we should have been literally starved. When at last we did get a wagon-load of supplies, they were served out in the usual head-over-heels fashion, in which the Cape authorities did everything. An hour before a start on a long patrol raw flour, green coffee, and freshly-killed meat would be distributed. By this clever arrangement the government saved a large quantity of provisions. The men would only draw a part. What was the good of taking the rations when there was no time either for making bread, cooking the meat, or roasting the coffee? An order came out that no back rations, though over due, would be issued. Any remonstrances were met by the rejoinder, What are you growling at? are you not getting free rations? Now that is exactly what we were not doing, for we were getting little or no rations at all. On several occasions the men refused to move out of camp until proper food had been supplied; and this shows how the authorities knew they were to blame, no notice having been at the time, or subsequently, taken of this mutinous behaviour. I do not hesitate to say, that the entire force would have been much better off if they had not had these so-called free rations. The officers of the different troops had never as yet failed in this one point. Wherever the police had been moved to they always arranged that wagon-loads of food should meet them somewhere or other. Before this war starvation was an exception, now it had become the rule. Several people followed up the force after a time, marching with wagons containing liquors and provisions; but they charged exorbitantly for everything. Brandy of the worst kind, known in the colony as "cape smoke," at ten shillings a bottle, small biscuits at twopence each, tinned salmon and meat, the tins containing about four ounces, at five shillings. Such things of course were not obtainable by the police on their pay, but sometimes we were obliged to buy in order to keep body and soul together.

These grievances lasted long and were indeed endless. I will not trouble the reader by enumerating more of them. From the beginning to the end of the war, it was quite a chance that the Colonial forces were fed, when the Colonial commissariat had anything to do with providing the necessary supplies. When we came to be fed from the Imperial commissariat, as was eventually the case, we had more than enough good food and to spare, and not only necessaries, but oftentimes luxuries. We did not ask for, nor did we expect, luxuries, but we surely had a right to all that was really necessary. The authorities boasted all the time that we were having free rations, made this an excuse for interfering with the arrangements of the police officers, who, to do them justice, had always in the old times seen that we were fed. Men cannot fight without food, and we were no exception to the rule.

In addition to the neglect from which we suffered in this respect, we had no money. The troops were not paid up at the end of the month, as they had been before, and in accordance with the agreement; but when we were paid, the colonial government calmly ignored the fifth clause of the agreement, and stopped £5 a month from us, on the excuse, as they pretended, that they were supplying us with *free* rations. But this is only one of the many times that they broke both the word and the spirit of the agreement we had signed.

Quantities of arms and ammunition were daily arriving at Ibeka. These supplies were due, not to the foresight of the Colonial authorities, but to the general, who had retained these arms against his orders from home. He had repeatedly asked, it appeared afterwards, the Colonial government to purchase these arms, but without success. It was fortunate for the colony that the general acted as he did, or the state to which the Colonial forces would have been reduced without arms or ammunition it is not difficult to imagine. These arms of which I am speaking were those which had been exchanged for Martini-Henrys, at that time the new arms of the Imperial service.

I will now return to the proceedings which took place subsequently to the fight at Ibeka. Two days after the memorable Sunday when we finally beat off the Galekas, some Fingoes brought in the head of 'Nita, the famous "witch doctor" of Kreli. Her body some hours afterwards was also brought in. She it was who led the Galekas to make the attack at Ibeka. Her body was tattooed nearly all over, and her legs and arms were covered with small chains, brass rings, and leather straps. She also *doctored* the army, giving each man a piece of hair string, with some bits of wood attached, to hang round their necks, as a charm against the bullets of the white man. It was 'Nita too who had caused

Lindenxoxa, the second and favourite son of Kreli, to be put to death, on the supposition that he had prevented the Galekas from beating us by some magic or other on his part.

Such was the account given of 'Nita by some Galeka prisoners. I think it more than probable that Lindenxoxa was killed, because he was the only one of Kreli's sons and councillors who did not want war, and who always used his influence to prevent it as much as possible. For some reason, however, he was put out of the way, being first starved for several days, and then beaten nearly to death, and buried alive with what little life was left in him.

It was a wonderful face, this great witch doctor's, full of energy and power; even as you looked at it in death, you could see strength of character in every line of it. The mastery this woman must have obtained over the chiefs of her tribes, to become the powerful enchantress she was during her entire lifetime! And this was her death! Her head was packed in a rocket box full of lime, and sent down to King William's Town.

The day after this little episode we were visited by the Tambookie chief, Gangeleswe. He was dressed in European clothes, and escorted by about fifty of his principal chiefs. This chief is the most cowardly, contemptible nigger in the whole of South Africa; in fact, I doubt if his equal in these respects is to be found in any country or any clime. His latest achievement had been to almost beat one of his wives to death; but as I have to speak about him a little further on, I will leave him for the present, except to say that he stayed all that night, and after an interview with Commandant Griffiths left for his country.

That same day two men came in from the enemy with a flag of truce. They had come from Mapassa, a Galeka chief of considerable importance in his own tribe. There is no doubt that his men had been all fighting both at the Guadana, and Ibeka; but they now said he did not wish to fight, and that neither he nor his men had fought. I believe he personally had not, but there is not the slightest doubt that his men were in both battles, and it is now a well-known fact, that the principal part of his men joined the Gaikas in their rebellion, and aided both the Galekas and Gaikas all through the war.

They requested to be taken over by the government, and were allowed to cross the Kei with their cattle, guns, and *assegais*. They camped on some land not far from Impetu, and there formed in the very heart of the frontier a most formidable headquarters for all the rebellious natives in the colony. Their women kept their friends well supplied with ammunition and all necessaries, and also fully acquainted with all our movements and any of our plans on which they could obtain information.

It is inconceivable that any government could, in the first place, have allowed them to retain their arms; and in the second place, have posted them where they did, right in the line of communication between one tribe already at war with us and another tribe on the point of rebellion. But so it was.

Botman, Kreli's chief councillor, told me two years afterwards, that this move had been planned by Kreli himself; that Kreli knew the English never refused to take over a tribe, and that if they could only be placed where they eventually were, they would be most useful to him, as no doubt they were. I don't pretend to declare positively whether this was so or not; I give it as it was told me by Botman, and for what it is worth. If true, it certainly was a very wily scheme of that cunning old Galeka chieftain, Kreli.

We were now getting ready for another move. Rumour said we were to prepare for an attack on the "Great Place" of Kreli. The Fingoes were being armed and divided under different officers, and attached to different columns of the forces. Every preparation was being made for a lengthened march. Major Elliot was organizing a force of Tembus close to Umtata. He had with him No. 6 troop F. A. M. Police, the Queenstown Volunteers, and a few burghers and Fingoes. This force was to operate on the other side of the Bashee, a tolerably large river about 22 miles from Ibeka, and the eastern boundary of Galekaland. His force never amounted to more than 250 white men and 3000 Tembus, the latter quite useless, and with this corps he was instructed to cut off any of the enemy that were driven by us from the westward. How our two forces fared I shall relate in my next chapter.

CHAPTER 9

Kreli's Kraal

Owing to want of sufficient ammunition and supplies, we had wasted nine or ten valuable days. In the mean time the Galekas were strengthening their armies by reinforcements from several tribes that were supposed to be at peace with us, notably the Gaikas and Bomvanas. In fact, any Kaffir who wanted to have a fight joined the Galekas, who asked no questions. The enemy were daily augmenting their forces at Kreli's "Great Place;" and at length about fifty of our volunteers, who were out on a foraging expedition some few miles from Ibeka, had a brush with the enemy; two of our number were severely wounded, but their comrades managed to bring them in.

A day or two after this the Galekas began to come in sight of our camp, and fire off guns and dance about as a sort of challenge for us to attack them. They had had some experience of us at Ibeka, and so they would not come to close quarters. We let them alone, contenting ourselves with occasionally sending a few men out and taking a few shots at them, when, as we presumed they would, they generally decamped, though sometimes returning the fire. At last our commandant determined to make a regular attack on Kreli's "Great Place." The volunteers and the police were getting restless, and the former were discontented at being detained in camp doing nothing, with the niggers so close at hand.

On an early evening two-thirds of the force at Ibeka, with two guns, were ordered to start at daylight next morning. We were also ordered to take two days' rations with us.

At daylight we started, and an hour afterwards a thick fog came on, and we were obliged to return.

On the following clay we again started at two o'clock in the morning, slowly wending our way towards our destination.

Let me now describe, as well as I can, the country and the place we were going to attack. The reader will recollect by referring to the last plan, the small stream there marked as intersecting the slope in front of Barnett's house, separating a portion of the incline from the stony ridge on the left. Five hundred yards to the right of this, and running parallel with the small stream, and directly towards the coast, is a road leading to one of the trading-stations in Galekaland. We proceeded along this road, and after progressing about six miles turned suddenly off to our left. This brought us to a very steep hill, up which we had to go, across the *veldt*.

A short distance from the top we halted, and the various troops commenced to take up the positions assigned to them. The artillery and a troop of volunteers were advanced to the top of the hill. The remainder of the volunteers were sent round to the extreme right of the artillery; and about a mile from them to the left the remainder of the police were posted. One police troop, No. 3, numbering 80 men, was held in reserve for emergencies. We were all to advance simultaneously at the sound of the bugle.

While waiting for this, let me describe, as I afterwards saw it, Kreli's Kraal, or "Great Place," the habitation of this redoubtable chief, the most powerful in Kaffirland. The hill we were now on was grassy and ascended to a point, and thence descended by a gentle slope for about 700 yards to the Xoxa River, which runs immediately past the *kraal*. This river flows past Kreli's hut, right at the foot of a perpendicular *krantz* or hill, for about half-a-mile. Immediately under the steepest part of this *krantz*, but on the same side of the river as we were posted, stood the hut of Kreli, surrounded by several others. Here and there a few large thorn-trees were dotted about. The ground is very uneven. Only one way was to be seen by which the enemy could escape. By following the course of the river for about a mile and a half, a flat opened out, leading to the Manubie Forest and the coast. There was no other line of retreat. We had not, unfortunately, sufficient force to block this outlet, but it was commanded by the guns through the whole distance. We were now waiting for the arrival of the Fingoes, who reached us after some little delay. They were directed to go round the foot of the hill on which we were posted, and then proceed to the left with a view, if possible, of driving the enemy into the arms of the volunteers, who were placed on the right, expressly to wait for them. A troop of police accompanied the Fingoes. The commandant with his trumpeter only rode to the top of the hill, and we anxiously awaited the bugle sound which was to be our signal for making the attack.

It was at this time just getting daylight, and there was every appearance of a fine day for the pretty stiff work we had in hand.

A few shots were soon heard, and the bugle sounded the advance. The guns were driven up the remainder of the hill at a gallop, unlimbered and came into action, firing shrapnel shell at the *kraals* and huts. The volunteers, police, and Fingoes dismounted, and commenced independent firing about 200 yards off. The Galekas were completely taken by surprise, they only fired a few shots, and then turned and fled for the outlet, which I have already described, along the course of the river. The entire force, except the gun escorts and the troop of police held in reserve, pursued them for three or four miles, the big guns continually firing as opportunity offered. When the Galekas reached the flat I have before indicated, they turned and made a stand for about ten minutes, but as our men were gradually getting round them, and at the same time kept up a heavy firing on them, they were unable to hold the position they had taken, and speedily fled for the bush. The "retire" was now sounded, and the force was gradually brought back to the place where the guns were standing and had remained since morning. Why the guns were not used in the pursuit I am unable to say. They were well horsed, and the gunners were well trained, the road was flat, and they would have been of the greatest use in clearing the niggers from the various bushes. The escort and police troop being kept in reserve, prevented these men from being utilized to advantage, as unquestionably they might have been.

After a hard day's work we returned to Ibeka, the entire force thoroughly dissatisfied, and every one growling that we had not been allowed to pursue the enemy to the end. Had this been done there and then, as it might have been, the war would have been finished; such a blow would have been struck that the government would have been able to make their own terms with the Kaffirs. It is well known now that Kreli wanted to make peace after his *kraal* was destroyed, but by some bungling on the part of the authorities at Ibeka, he was never allowed the opportunity. He had lost some 300 men at Guadana some 1000 more at Ibeka, and about 250 more in the last fight. He saw his tribe being broken up without any diminution of the white men, and naturally enough he did not care to pursue further such a very one-sided game. As matters are, though he has been driven out of his country, he has never been thoroughly subdued. What has the country to show for it, after all the expenditure it has made in pursuing this chief and his tribe?

The government has nominally obtained possession of Galekaland, where it has placed a few European emigrants, and given location to a few hundred natives, supposed to be loyal. These natives have already been largely augmented by more of their countrymen, Galekas who have been driven out of their country. They are multiplying in very considerable numbers, and in the course of a few years, allied with one of Kreli's sons or grandsons, will again have become strong enough to try issues with the colonial government, though probably with no better success, but with the certainty, notwithstanding, of costing the government at the time, whenever it happens, a large amount of money, to say nothing of lives.

To return to the burning of Kreli's Kraal. Our loss amounted to two Fingoes killed, three wounded, two policemen wounded slightly, and three horses which were shot, two men of Bowker's Rovers wounded, one severely. This small number of casualties, in comparison with the loss sustained by the enemy, was trifling, and the moral effect on the enemy was proportionately great.

The defeat plainly taught them they could not stand against us, even in their own country, or in a stronghold which they had selected. If we had but followed them up, as I have suggested, the war would certainly have been at an end. Why this was not done it is difficult to say. The excuse was that there was little ammunition and less food. Of my own personal knowledge I can state there was plenty of ammunition available had they chosen to follow up the Kaffirs at the time; but as I had nothing to do with the commissariat department, I must take it there was not sufficient food, or else that the transport was inadequate. Why the want of food should have stopped the forces from proceeding I could never understand. When we eventually started we were not one whit better supplied. While we remained at Ibeka the troops were fed; when we left, they were not fed. To say that Commandant Griffiths could not proceed for want of ammunition and supplies may appear a reasonable excuse, but it was groundless. To say that he could not proceed with the force because the Colonial government had not sense and ability to organize a proper system of transport supply, and communication, would be more correct. I believe there was something behind the scenes that we knew nothing about. I refer to what was to be gathered from some correspondence which was afterwards published. The purport of the instructions from Cape Town as it appeared, was that the Galekas were to be permitted to scatter and divide, if so inclined. Any way, whether this report were correct or not, it is certain that for the rest of the war, on several occasions, we were marched day and night until we arrived close up to, and in some cases were actually surrounded by, the enemy, but we were always ordered to stop, thus giving them time to get away. This did not happen once only, but over and over again; and as the authorities were in no wise indisposed to send us out without provisions on other occasions, I cannot see why they should have hesitated in this instance. I can therefore only regard this marked neglect of opportunity as indicating great incompetency on the part either of our officers or of the government. Of course there was great discontent at these unsatisfactory proceedings amongst the volunteers and burghers. Many of these declared they came out "to fight, and not to play the fool." Many of them threatened to go home, and some of them actually did withdraw. Who can blame them? They were not fed or looked after in any way by the government, which did nothing beyond giving them ammunition. Had it not been for private supplies and wagons which the volunteers and burghers brought with them, they would have been starved on more than one occasion. They were a liberal lot of fellows, and the police were often-times indebted to them for a meal and a glass of grog.

After wasting about twelve days of valuable time, during which no wagons either of ammunition or food arrived from head-quarters, though I beg the reader to observe we were *waiting* for supplies, we left for a place called Lusisi in Galekaland. There bad been a trading-station here, but of course the house and outbuildings had been burnt, as had every other trading-station in Galekaland. We passed through Kreli's Kraal, or rather the place were the *kraal* had stood, and proceeded in a very cautious manner.

Very little was known of the part to which we were going. A trader who had been there was away in the colony, and we only had Fingoes for guides. Lusisi is about thirty-five miles from Ibeka. The road is good, passing through beautiful rolling pastures, intersected with small streamlets, with here and there a small wood or bush.

When we had proceeded about twenty miles from Ibeka, we formed a camp on a hill. Instead of proceeding at once to Lusisi, where it was well known the enemy were collecting again in force, we wasted three more days waiting to see if the imaginary supplies were coming. We had left Ibeka with seven days' rations in our saddle-bags, and as it turned out we were to have no more for another ten days. The saving to the government was of course large, as it stands to reason, if you can make about 2000 men subsist for seventeen days on the rations of seven days, a very considerable saving must be effected, at the expense of the men. On the fourth day after we left Ibeka, we broke up our camp and proceeded on our march to our destination.

We saw the scouts of the enemy on the surrounding hills, but nothing happened that day. We camped on our arrival, in the form of a square, the wagons which had brought the tents being placed on one side of the formation, with our three 7-pounder guns in the middle.

The spot selected for this camp was about the worst that could have possibly been chosen. The ground dipped down in a sort of scoop, so that two sides of the camp were in the centre of this scoop or hollow, making a water-course right through the camp; in fact, the two sides were, in the rain which soon followed, immersed in water to the depth of several inches. These sides were sheltered, the one by a thick bush and the other by a tolerably close growth of trees. The other two sides faced rising ground, which limited the view to about two miles. Such was the place our officers had chosen for a camp. By the time we had pitched our tents, and cooked and eaten our suppers, it was dark. About nine that evening it began to rain in a way peculiar to South Africa—buckets full at a time.

Pickets and sentries were posted for the night. The horses were brought inside the camp and " rung," and so begun our first night in Galekaland.

CHAPTER 10

Battle of Lusisi

The next morning, soon after daylight, the outlying pickets came in, reporting that the enemy was approaching. We were all turned out and placed in extended order round the camp. Two troops of police, with three troops of volunteers, were ordered out, dismounted, to take the direction of the bush I have before mentioned as being close to the camp. This detachment formed the front. On our extreme right about five hundred Kaffirs were seen coming down towards us, and shortly afterwards firing began. The enemy nearly surrounded the camp. For some time heavy firing was kept up on both sides. We were unable to use the big guns, the Fingoes being in the bush trying to drive the Galekas out.

After firing with our small arms for about a couple of hours, the Galekas, from some unexplained reason, suddenly ceased firing and ran, the Fingoes, volunteers, and police pursuing a short distance; but the rain coming down very hard, and making a very thick mist, these detachments were recalled. After they returned news was brought to the camp that some of the enemy had taken shelter in a cave, and that they were supposed to be chiefs. Two of the Fingoe leaders, brothers named Goss, went with a party of their men to get the Galekas out. The place they were in was close by a small stream, the course of which, turning at right angles towards the cave, made a sort of passage with high walls towards it. To reach the cave where these Galekas were concealed we had to go right up the stream, and then the mouth of the cave was visible, about as high as a man's head.

From the roof of the cave to the ground above there was not more than about two feet. The Fingoes went in first, and as they reached that part of the stream which was in view of the cave, were all shot dead. William Goss then went in with three more Fingoes, and these as they came in sight were also shot dead. Poor Goss was shot right through the heart. Two more Fingoes and Michael Goss then went in; the Fingoes were shot as soon as they appeared, and Michael Goss was wounded in the arm. He went forward a few yards calling for some more men. Two more came into this passage of death, when Michael Goss and one of the two men who had joined him were shot dead; the other ran outside again.

Allan Maclean and his Fingoes had now arrived on the spot, and he tried to get in with two of his men. One was shot, and he himself had a narrow escape, a bullet going through his sleeve and grazing his arm. They wisely retreated, and as only three, or at most four, men could get into the place at once, he resolved to try other measures. They first commenced to fire volleys from a hill about a hundred and fifty yards off, which commanded the entrance of the cave, but this only drove the enemy further back into it.

A Fingoe now climbed up on the bank, right above the cave, armed with an *assegai*. A stick was then cut and a hat put on it. Now, as only one man could come out of the cave at a time, to fire, they felt pretty sure of getting one, so they put the stick with the hat on it, round the corner. A party of men were in readiness to rush into the cave directly the shot had been fired from it. A nigger came out of the cave to fire at the hat, and was immediately stabbed right through the neck by the Fingoe above, and in the confusion that followed, the party rushed in and killed the remainder of the men inside. There were seven in all, Galekas. On our side we lost eleven Fingoes, and the brothers Goss, who, poor fellows, both left widows and large families. We buried them the next morning, with military honours, and thus in the middle of Kaffirland they found their graves. Both were frontier farmers, living right upon the further border by the Umtata River, thoroughly good, honest fellows, universally liked and respected by all who knew them. This was the last fight, such as it was, we had with the Galekas for some time. They scattered themselves all over the country, and we had long and tedious patrols driving them through the territory.

Our camp was now in a fearful condition; three days it had been raining hard without intermission. All the tents in the hollows stood in several inches of water, in spite of the deep trenches we had dug all round them. All the men were wet through, and when they came off sentry duty in that state, had only these miserable, comfortless tents for shelter. Our rations hail been all used up for two days, and not a sign appeared of any arriving. Meat was served out, but as everything was saturated, a fire could not be lighted so as to cook it. If by chance a fire did get lighted and fairly started, the heavy downpour of rain immediately put it out. So our poor tired and hungry men were forced to satisfy themselves with a little raw meat and such *mealies* as the Fingoes now and then gave them. In addition to this, one night we had a false alarm, and were out the whole night in the wind and rain, waiting for an expected attack which never came. For five days it rained incessantly, with the heavy downpour I have described. We continued without food, and having to sit on our saddles, in order to keep out of the water, and consequently without sleep, except such as we could get seated in this fashion. It is a mercy the Galekas had cleared out, for we were so utterly done and exhausted by fatigue, privation, and starvation, that the whole camp would easily have fallen a prey into their hands, had they attacked us in the condition we were then in.

When at length the rain ceased, we were ordered to be ready to start one afternoon as soon as the tents were dry. As we had had nothing to eat except raw meat and uncooked *mealies* for six days, we informed the authorities of our intention not to budge an inch until we had some food served out to us. The officers at first tried persuasion, then bullying and threatening, but the men remained firm; if, as the officers alleged, there was no food to give them, they would remain where they were until some arrived; start they would not. At last one of the officers went to the commandant about the matter, and after more expostulation, a wagon-load of provision was bought from a sutler who had followed up the forces; and we had three days' groceries served out to us, and were warned to start the next morning. We were told that the ringleaders of this last movement were known, and that they would be dealt with at a future date, at which of course we laughed. The writer knew the so-called ringleaders in this instance, and he knows also that they were never afterwards interfered with; the authorities thus admitting themselves in the wrong.

While we were at Lusisi, being half-drowned and nearly starved, Major Elliot, with the force under his command, had taken up a position at Fort Bowker. This fort was an old one built by our late commandant in the first Galeka war, fifteen years before. Little remained of it at the present time, a few mounds being the only indications that a building or fort had once existed. Close by was a large trading-station, which had been destroyed by the Galekas at the beginning of the war.

Fort Bowker was distant about twenty-five miles east of Guadana Hill, and some twenty miles from the mouth of the Bashee River.

The plan of the campaign on which we were now entering, to complete the dispersal of the enemy, was this: we were to spread out in three columns from Lusisi, marching towards Fort Bowker, driving the Galekas in front of us, where Major Elliot's column would pounce down on them. A good many of the volunteers and Fingoes went home at this time, and when we started we had only about 500 police, 1200 volunteers and burghers, and between 400 and 500 Fingoes. We divided this force into three columns, one taking way by the sea, another a road ten miles inland, and the third a road about twenty-five miles inland. There was thus about twelve miles between the columns.

In the day-time we extended; at night we formed a camp. A 7-pounder gun went with each column. The whole force advanced with the greatest difficulty, having to ford rivers, being sometimes without food, and in other ways suffering the greatest privations. We, however, made a clean sweep of Galekaland, driving the Kaffirs in front of us, and capturing large quantities of cattle and sheep.

We occupied about eighteen days going through the country in the manner I have described; and when we reached Fort Bowker, we were all more or less exhausted with the hardships we had undergone. Many were sick with fever and dysentery, and every one needed a rest. The commandant halted at Fort Bowker, and we pitched our camp. Here we obtained provisions, and stopped for some six weeks, making occasionally short patrols, to feel the whereabouts of the enemy if we could find them. But by this time the Galekas had all, or nearly all, crossed the Bashee, and had taken refuge with the Bomvanas, driving with them such cattle as they could get over.

The burghers now wanted to return, and there was no law to keep them against their will, so the last detachment of them left us and returned home, taking with them the share of cattle which fell to their lot. We were marched back to Ibeka, not being strong enough to maintain the position we had taken. Major Elliot's column returned to Tembuland, as things seemed to be getting quieter.

All the men of experience foretold that the Galekas would recross the Bashee into their own country directly the force at Fort Bowker was withdrawn. This, sure enough, they did, and before six weeks had elapsed after our arrival at Ibeka, the country was alive with them again.

More volunteers were now brought up from the colony, and with the addition which this made to our force, we started again, going over nearly the same ground, and sometimes in the same manner, working in conjunction with Major Elliot's column. This time we went across the Bashee, and right down to the mouth of the Umtata River through Bomvanaland, capturing many thousand head of cattle.

The Galekas this time broke through into Pondoland, and as the volunteers again wished to go back, we were obliged to return to Ibeka. During these two trips right through Galekaland we had had no fighting of any importance; but the men had undergone many trials and hardships, and a large proportion of them became sick. A hospital had been formed at Butterworth, and to this our men were now sent. It remained the hospital during the war, and was well conducted by an experienced English medical man, who was in charge with well-qualified assistants.

After this last patrol of the police, the Cape government declared it was perfectly certain the Galekas would remain quiet. In the same way as before the beginning of hostilities, the government would listen to no one. They would hear of no one knowing anything about the matter but themselves. Meetings were being held again in all the frontier towns, as well as at Graham's Town and King William's Town. At these public meetings the conduct of the Cape government was strongly and unreservedly denounced, and the governor was petitioned to assemble parliament on the frontier instead of at Cape Town.

All this time the Gaikas were known to be on the very point of breaking into rebellion, and the folly of not disarming Mapassa when he was located in the colony was now seen.

The Cape government resolved that his tribe should be disarmed, but sent no more than between forty and fifty police on this service. The result was easy to be foreseen. McKinnon, one of the chiefs, refused to give up his arms. The police retired, not being in sufficient numbers to compel the arms to be surrendered; and during the night McKinnon fled, followed by very nearly all Mapassa's tribe, making his way to Sandilli, and there fraternized with the Gaikas.

This event happened towards the latter end of November, and though the Gaikas were not in open rebellion, they were only waiting their time till the Galekas should get back into their own country, to which they were daily flocking in great numbers.

There were not enough forces in the Transkei to continue regularly patrolling the country, and it was an indisputable fact, that unless the country was steadily and continuously patrolled, all the work of clearing the territory for the last four months would be thrown away. We were constantly, therefore, on the move from Ibeka, but the force was so small that the Galekas gradually slipped in.

A battle was now fought about twelve miles from Ibeka, in which our men so narrowly escaped being beaten that the country was completely roused. Public meetings were again held everywhere, vigilance committees were formed, and all the frontier towns were prepared for defence. Farmers and their families were *trekking* into *laager*. Everywhere there were protests of the strongest character against the way in which the Cape government was acting. At a large public meeting held at Kei-road, the loyal inhabitants threatened to take the law into their own hands, and shoot every nigger found on their farms. As they were all being ruined day by day, and losing their stock by theft, their complaints were not without good foundation. How the ministry at the Cape were, in consequence of their mismanagement, dismissed by the Governor is now a matter of history, and I will at once relate the details of the battle to which I have just alluded.

CHAPTER 11

Battle of Umzintzani

On the road leading towards the mouth of the River Kei from Ibeka, there was a place called Holland's Shop, a large trading-station; but at this time the whole station had been burned to the ground. A party of volunteers, consisting of infantry from Port Elizabeth, with one gun of the Cape Town Artillery, and one gun of the Graham's Town Artillery, together with No. 9 Troop F. A. M. Police, left Ibeka on one of our customary patrols. This small force was under the command of Captain Bayley, who had recently been the adjutant of the 9th Regiment of Foot, and who afterwards became our colonel, when the F. A. M. P. were converted into the C. M. R. Our division had marched on with the police troop, forming an advance guard, when we suddenly came upon the Galekas in force. Inspector Bourne sent back at once a messenger to Captain Bayley, who brought his party forward at a double, and the whole of our force then took up a position on a small hill just abreast of the ruins of Holland's Shop.

This occurred about three o'clock in the afternoon of the 2nd of December.

Whilst the infantry and artillery were getting into position, the police were engaged in doing a little desultory skirmishing.

The Galekas were in great force, rapidly increasing in numbers on a ridge about half-a-mile off.

Exactly opposite this ridge runs a small river called the Nabaxa. Along the banks of this, about half-a-mile nearer the sea, was a deep *kloof* or valley, out of which they could be seen coming up in great numbers.

The police now advanced, and at something like 250 yards from the enemy commenced firing. The Graham's Town gun, which was well horsed, drove down to the assistance of the police, unlimbered, came into action, and peppered the niggers right merrily.

In the meanwhile the Cape artillery and the infantry were not idle. The artillery sent shell after shell into the bush, and the infantry fired at the enemy as the shells drove them out of their cover. They were thus forced out of the *kloof*, but effected a junction with their friends on the ridge. At this point part of them divided, and under cover of the ridge started off to outflank us.

A party of police were despatched to stop this manoeuvre, and then the rest of the niggers charged right down the hill from the ridge, on to the gun and remnant of police that were left with it. There were not more than twenty police, and about eleven or twelve of the artillery. The Galekas who charged us numbered between 400 and 500. When they reached within a hundred and fifty yards, the order was given us to retire; the police mounted and retired except three men, whose horses had broken loose. Two of them reached the gun in safety, but the third, Wellesley, was unfortunately shot in the hip, and was almost immediately *assegaied*. Though on his knees he fought hard, and killed four Kaffirs before they finally despatched him.

Several of the enemy were shot by the police and artillery, as they clustered round the poor fellow, stabbing him to death.

Lieutenant Wells, who was in command of the Graham's Town gun, waited until the natives were within fifty or sixty yards of his piece, and then fired a case shot into the midst of them. In the confusion that ensued the gun was limbered up, and retired at a gallop, with the two policemen, up a steep hill and rejoined the rest of our party.

The enemy did not immediately come on again; but about five o'clock, or two hours before sunset, they again collected and charged the camp.

The two guns now poured several rounds of case shot into them as they advanced, which they did to within a hundred and fifty yards, where they were able to take shelter behind some stones and ant-heaps, and from this position one man of the Port Elizabeth volunteers was shot dead. This was almost the only casualty that occurred up to this time.

It was now sunset, but with the moon well up it continued tolerably light. The enemy every now and again advanced *en masse,* and poured a volley or two into the camp, wounding some of our side. They made a final charge about nine o'clock, coming close up to the guns, howling and firing independently; but finding our return fire too warm for them, they retired again into the *kloof,* and were seen no more that night.

Some Fingoes joined the camp during the same night, and the next morning went out as usual to kill the wounded men who were left.

The loss to the enemy was between seventy and eighty killed, and we heard afterwards that from 150 to 200 wounded were removed during the night, as is their custom. The loss on our side was two killed, with four police and three volunteers wounded.

The wounded were sent in during the day to Ibeka, and a permanent camp was formed about 300 yards from the scene of the battle.

Large reinforcements of police were now sent out from Ibeka, and frequent patrols went from this place, now called Umzintzani from the name of a small river which flows close by. These patrols were constantly coming across small bodies of the enemy, who fled, after firing a few shots, at our approach.

At this time it became known that the Galekas were coming back into their country for the third time. They had left the greater part of their women and all their cattle with the Bomvanas across the Bashee; but all their fighting men had again taken the field, and were supposed to be under the command of Sigow.

This chief certainly bore a charmed life. He had been wounded several times, and very often with difficulty escaped capture. He was notorious for his intense hatred of the white men, and was a brave and intelligent man. The Cape government at this crisis tried to bring the burghers and volunteers again to the front. They had both been so badly treated on previous occasions when they had been called out, that they one and all of them this time refused to come. The war minister attributed their refusal to the circumstance that they were to be placed under the command of Imperial officers. It is more than surprising how any such statement could have been made. These branches of the Colonial service were only too glad to be placed under officers who knew how to command and use them, instead of the incompetent leaders who had previously had charge of them. They were not, however, after all called out; and in the early part of December, the volunteers having all returned to their colony, some of Her Majesty's troops were marched over the Kei River to Ibeka. From this point their orders were to begin, with the police, the task of once more for the third time clearing Galekaland.

I have already related how some of the Imperial forces had been, for some time previous to this, occupying Pullen's Farm, Impetu, and Komgha. These troops were now moved up to Ibeka, part of the 88th taking their places at the posts they left. A Naval Brigade also marched to Ibeka with two guns and two 24-pounder rocket tubes. A corps of infantry named Pulleine's Rangers, and a corps of light cavalry called Carrington's Light Horse, were raised in the colony for service. The first-mentioned corps was commanded by Major Pulleine, and the latter by Lieutenant Carrington, both of the 24th regiment. These two corps did excellent service. The Infantry acted as garrisons at the various points we occupied whilst marching through Galekaland on this third occasion. Fifty men of the 24th were also mounted, under Lieutenant Clements, and acted as cavalry with the column under the command of Colonel Glyn.

By Christmas Day we had formed a camp within two miles of our old camping-ground at Lusisi, and were making preparations for marching once more over the territory.

The police were now under the Imperial authorities, and we all welcomed the beneficial change. We had plenty to eat, with sufficient time for meals, and we went over the ground quite as rapidly, if not more so than before, and we always contrived to camp in daylight instead of dark.

If any of my readers have campaigned they will know the difference made in the comfort of a camp by what I have mentioned.

While we are camped and waiting the orders to march, let me turn to notice some events which were happening on the other side of the Kei.

Kiva, let me first remark, one of the most noted of the Galeka warriors, had broken through into the colony, burning every store and farm-house on his way, and had joined the Gaikas, who were now in open rebellion. The communication from the Kei road and Komgha was blocked, and a policeman was shot whilst carrying despatches between these two places. A body of forty police, under charge of an officer carrying the government despatches, was attacked and forced to retreat. At length Major Moore, with a detachment of the 88th and some twenty of the police, whilst escorting the mails, had a severe fight with the Galekas. The engagement lasted over two hours. We lost in it three men killed and several wounded, and a cart-load of ammunition, and narrowly escaped defeat, through the whole of his own force bolting. The major managed, however, to lay the fault on the police, who were invariably made the scapegoats if any failure occurred. The V. C. was given to him for some act of gallantry in this remarkable action, and eventually he was made commandant of our force. His report of the action and the account given by a sergeant of the police engaged, who carried a man off the field on his own horse, differed very much. According to the statement of the police, the soldiers ran first, and the police followed them.

I am afraid we did not appreciate Major Moore as highly as he estimated himself. He was slightly wounded in the wrist. The enemy in this fight were led by McKinnon, who had escaped when the disarmament of his tribe was attempted.

I will now return to our camp in the Transkei. The day following Christmas Day we proceeded on our march. We were greatly extended, and on this occasion were divided into two columns. One column was placed under the command of Captain Upcher, and the other, or head-quarters column, under Colonel Glyn.

We marched over exactly the same ground as before, encountering the same difficulties of transport, and several times meeting the enemy, who made at no time any but a very weak and brief defence, and then fled. We captured immense herds of cattle. On one occasion about 1200 women fell into our hands, and were sent into Ibeka. These poor things were in the most awful state of destitution from long hunger. They had been for some time living on the bark of trees, and such roots as they could grub up.

We returned ourselves to Ibeka on the 10th of January, 1878, having for the third time completely cleared Galekaland.

During this patrol we had done on an average thirty miles a day, and had been well fed and looked after, and what we certainly appreciated, well employed. The hard work that fell to our lot we did not mind. Great, we found, was the contrast between the Imperial and Colonial authorities; for with the latter we had an overwhelming measure of work, but no food; while with the former the balance was well adjusted.

We were not allowed to rest quietly for any length of time. Two days after our return on this occasion the troops were all again ordered out. Our destination was a place about seven miles from Ibeka, called Leslie's mission station. We were sent in consequence of the Galekas, who had not long before crossed into Gaikaland, having recrossed the Kei. They were reported to be assembling in large numbers close to the river and near its mouth.

From the camp at Leslie's mission an advanced camp was formed, at a place called N'amaxa, under the command of Major Owen of the 88th. Both at Leslie's mission and N'amaxa a mixed force was stationed, as it was uncertain which place the Galekas would attack. Eventually we discovered they determined to attack the advanced camp at N'amaxa.

At this station we had a company of the 24th. another of the 88th, with fifty men of the Naval Brigade, two troops of police, and two 7-pounder guns, with detachments of the police artillery.

I have reason to think the enemy chose to attack this camp,

because of the excellent cover they could reach if defeated. The surrounding country was undulating, but on the river-side it presented a series of deep *kloofs*, affording capital shelter.

Immediately on the right was a long ridge, known as the Tala ridge, and on this the enemy were collecting and then disappearing into the *kloof* below us on our front.

About three o'clock the rocket battery commenced firing into the bush in front of us, as apparently by this time a large body of Galekas had collected. The enemy were quickly driven out of the bush, and began to form on each of our flanks. They then broke into skirmishing order and charged. On all sides they were met by a heavy and determined fire which arrested their progress. After standing still a while in this position, they were literally mown down by two guns of the Royal Artillery which had just arrived, and were now brought into action. The fire was so hot that the whole Galeka army was soon in full retreat to the bush.

The enemy were immediately pursued by the mounted men till dark; at sun-down the recall was sounded, and we had time to get some rest.

Sixty bodies of the enemy were found close to the camp, that is to say, within a hundred yards. Down the *kloof* on the left we counted forty-six more bodies, and several more were seen lying about in different directions, which we had not time to count. We estimated the loss of the enemy at 150 killed and 200 wounded. Our loss was confined to three men severely wounded, privates belonging to the 88th. One of these, poor fellow, was shot right through the jaw, the bullet going in one side of his face and passing out on the other, but he recovered. Three Galeka chiefs were killed in this action.

After this battle we saw nothing more of the enemy. We had a patrol of a few days along the Tala ridge in search of them, but we could discover none. During this time both men and horses suffered most cruelly from want of water. A part of the advanced camp was despatched to a place called Quintana, about twenty-two miles from Ibeka, and the remainder returned to Ibeka.

Constant patrols were considered to be still necessary, and we continued to erect forts in various parts of Galekaland, within easy distance of each other.

A sufficient body of men were stationed at each of these forts, and constant patrols being sent from them the country was at last effectually kept clear of Galekas.

This well-conceived plan, it is needless to remark, was the suggestion of the Imperial officer in command. The Colonial officers would never have thought of it, and had it been proposed, would have raised many objections. No doubt they would have proceeded as before, scouring the country from end to end, in no way bringing the war to a conclusion.

CHAPTER 12

Battle of Quintana

While these events were happening in the Transkei, three gentlemen—R. G. Tainton, John Tainton, and W. Brown—had been murdered by the Gaikas at a place called Berlin, about twelve miles from King William's Town.

These three gentlemen had been sent on a mission by the Cape government, with no other escort but a few black policemen, who, upon the Kaffirs attacking, one and all fled. The murderers were eventually taken and hanged.

The whole of the Gaikas, at this time under Sandilli, had risen in open rebellion. Several of the tribes of emigrant Tambookies in Tembuland were also on the point of rebellion. Various commands were out under Colonial officers, and generally war was raging along the whole frontier.

At Impetu a company of the 24th, under Captain Wardell, had been cut off from all communication and supplies, and it took a mixed force of close upon 700 men, with three 7-pounders under Colonel Lambert, to relieve their post.

Very nearly all the farmers round about Komgha, with their families, had taken refuge in *laager* at this station, where they suffered severely from exposure and privation. They were, however, after a brief interval, safely brought away from their perilous position.

The farmers through these events were of course heavy losers; all their houses had been burnt to the ground, and they had lost great quantities of stock. Those who had been relieved at Impetu were all placed in a fresh *laager* at Komgha, and there they were obliged to remain till the end of the war, when they returned to the wrecks of their former flourishing houses—all more or less ruined through the fault of a government which would not listen to the representations of the frontier farmers who had so justly expressed their alarm.

In the Transkei preparations were now being made for an attack on the Chichaba valley, where the Kaffirs, since their defeat at N'amaxa, had now collected in large numbers.

This beautiful valley, which is about thirteen miles long, and begins at a point opposite the ending of the Tala ridge, runs parallel with the River Kei, and towards its mouth. The valley abounded in very dense bushes, so thick in some places as to make it impossible for any one to move many yards in any direction. The only paths down to it—for roads there are none—are very rugged and precipitous. At this place we were to make our next attack. For this purpose two columns were formed on the Komgha side under the command of Colonel Lambert and Major Moore, and on the Transkei side a column under the orders of Colonel Glyn. The force on the Komgha side embodied about 250 white men, soldiers and police, with about 1200 Fingoes. On the Transkei side, on which I was, the forces consisted, of soldiers and police together, of about 360 white men with 250 Fingoes under Allan Maclean and Veldtman. After two or three reconnaissances to find out the exact whereabouts of the enemy, all three columns advanced, about the middle of January. The Transkei column proceeding along the Tala ridge, and the columns on the Komgha side marching through Impetu. The Kaffirs made little or no resistance, and after a week's desultory fighting and skirmishing, were completely driven out of the valley.

Between five and six thousand head of cattle and sheep were captured on the Komgha side by Colonel Lambert's column, after being driven out of the bush by Maclean's Fingoes. The guns and rockets did great service, and no doubt largely contributed to the success of the expedition.

Let me here make one or two remarks about captured cattle, which proved a source of great grumbling and discontent amongst the police. During the Galeka and Gaika wars, not less than 15,000 head of cattle and at least 20,000 sheep had been captured in various fights, in which the police had taken an active part. In most cases, in fact, the capture was due to this force alone. What became of these cattle no one was permitted to know. All were sent to Ibeka, and there herded and looked after by a party of Fingoes and white men, told off for this express purpose. Taking the value of the cattle at £3 per head, the whole number captured would represent a sum of about £45,000. If the sheep be computed at the low price of four shillings a piece, making £4,000, we have a grand total of about £49,000, and certainly this would be a low estimate; but I have put it low purposely, to allow for thefts, and deaths from various causes. Now the entire force of police employed in the warfare which I have detailed amounted to about 600 men, and they were fairly entitled to a third of the whole amount of £49,000. A third of this sum would be £16,333, which, divided equally amongst the 600 men, should have given each of us about £27. The reader may be inquisitive enough to ask how much the Frontier Armed and Mounted Police actually received? At the end of nine months, when the whole country had been quiet for some time, and we were settled in our new stations in the Transkei, the magnificent sum of £1-8s-4d was handed to each of us, as his share of prize money. As a mounted force, we had been mainly instrumental in capturing and driving these cattle and sheep, and this was our reward. Can it be wondered that great discontent prevailed? The authorities must have known that some persons had made a grand thing out of this. As the sum only of £800 was in all paid to the police, the revelation would be interesting into whose pocket went the remainder, say £15,533.

A famine had now come upon the Kaffirs. Hundreds of them were daily giving themselves up, and surrendering their arms to obtain food and get fat; and having accomplished these aims, they immediately rejoined their friends. No precautions were taken to detain them; no work was laid on them. They came in, said they were sorry, were forgiven, and allowed to follow their own devices. The major part of them, when refreshed and fatted up, rejoined the various chiefs to whom they belonged. This was afterwards demonstrated by numbers of the killed being found with "passes" on them from magistrates and other people authorized to give them.

A pass is a certificate that the native bearing this document is loyal, and is permitted to pass from one part of the colony to the other.

Towards the end of January the Gaikas and Galekas, under Kiva, Sigow, and McKinnon, were again gathering in the valley of the Kei, at the foot of the Tala ridge.

From information brought in by spies and others, it was known that they contemplated an attack upon some place or other, but the exact place could not then be indicated with any certainty. But as they were all getting very short of ammunition, it was supposed they would attack Ibeka, or Quintana, twenty-two miles distant from Ibeka. At both these places large quantities of ammunition and stores had been collected, the obtaining of which by the enemy would have been a grand stroke of good fortune for them, and a very serious loss to us. The ammunition and provisions accumulated at these places represented the entire stores available in the Transkei.

A strong detachment of police and two 7-pounders were sent on to Leslie's mission station, which lies about half-way between Ibeka and Quintana. This detachment was under the command of Captain Robinson, and was intended as a reserve, so that whichever of the two places the Kaffirs attacked, he could quickly move to its assistance.

At Ibeka two troops of police, with some companies of the 24th Regiment, and a party of Pulleine's Rangers, were stationed, with twenty-five men of Carrington's Light Horse. This force was strengthened with a 7-pounder of the Police Artillery, and a detachment of Royal Artillery with two 7-pounders, and of the Naval Brigade with two Armstrong guns.

The ground round Ibeka had been at various times strongly entrenched, and there was no fear of the Kaffirs successfully attacking this place. At Quintana a deep trench had been dug round the crown of a hill with out-lying rifle-pits and shelter trenches. The trench round the hill was about 400 yards long, and 300 yards broad. Inside this the tents were pitched, with the stores and ammunition piled in the centre.

The force stationed at Quintana consisted of three companies of the 24th, fifty men of Carringtons Light Horse, twenty-five men of Naval Brigade, with a 24-pounder rocket tube. One troop of police of sixty men, 9-pounder Police Artillery and eleven men, gun detachment; one 7-pounder Cape Town Artillery and nine men, gun detachment, with 200 Fingoes under Allan Maclean. Captain Upcher of the 24th was in command of the entire force.

We were not left long in suspense. Scouts from the enemy were seen on the surrounding hills about Quintana, and at last, through our spies, it was ascertained beyond doubt that the Kaffirs intended to attack this point.

Another police troop was despatched from Ibeka to Leslie's mission station, together with a company of Pulleine's Rangers.

I will now describe the place the Kaffirs were about to attack. The camp stood on a hill, three sides of which sloped down to the north-west and south, the fourth, or east side, was flat, the road from Ibeka leading into it. On the north side was a hill and a deep gully about half a mile off, and in the bottom of this again was a small stream. To the left and in a south-westerly direction was a level ground of about a mile in length, and then another hill, dotted about with thorn trees common to the country. In front or to the west was more level ground, interspersed with trees and shrubs, the ground generally was rugged and uneven, affording excellent cover for the enemy.

At daylight on the 7th of February, 1878, many of the enemy's scouts were again seen on the hills in front of us; the camp was called, all the tents struck, and the force stationed as follows: the 9-pounder was placed at the N.W. corner of the trench, the 7-pounder at the S.-W., with the 24-pounder rocket tube in the middle; Carrington's Horse on the right front; Fingoes on the left front; the 24th lined the trench immediately fronting the enemy, and the police were stationed on the east side, in case of the enemy trying to outflank us.

A heavy, drenching rain now came on, and speedily wetted every one through. About six o'clock in the morning the Light Horse, under Captain Carrington, with a few police and a company of the 24th, were sent out to try and draw the enemy on; this they did most successfully. On the Kaffirs came, some in columns and some skirmishing; the Light Horse and party retired into the camp as directed, where the remainder of our men had been kept out of sight in the trenches. The Kaffirs, evidently supposing that the party they had seen skirmishing was the entire force, advanced at a rapid pace across the *veldt*, charging directly for our camp. We computed the number to be about 4000.

When the enemy had reached within 500 yards our men quietly put their heads up out of the trenches, and commenced a heavy fire at the astonished Kaffirs, the big guns and the rocket tube at the same time opening fire. They stood this for about twenty minutes. They had tolerably good shelter, and a heavy mist was coming on, sometimes completely obscuring them from us; but after the expiration of about half-an-hour the fog fortunately lifted, and we discovered that they had crept within 150 yards of the trenches. A few rounds of case-shot, and some volleys from the Martini-Henrys, and they turned and fled, the Fingoes and Carringtons Horse after them, Carrington leading the way with a revolver and a stick, about 200 yards ahead of everyone else; these weapons he evidently considered good enough for chasing niggers with.

The police were also ordered to proceed with the rest; but owing to the obtuseness of their commanding officer, did not get away until too late to be of use. Captain Robinson's column came up when the enemy were in full retreat, and joined the pursuit. The 9-pounder also followed the flying enemy, getting some good shots at them. Round the camp the dead and dying were lying, the latter being speedily finished off by the Fingoes, after the custom of native warfare in Africa.

The casualties on our side amounted to three Fingoes killed, four wounded, two of Carrington's Horse wounded and their horses shot, and one policeman wounded. The loss to the enemy was about 300. For some days after this battle we had heavy burying fatigues.

This was the conclusion of the Galeka and Gaika wars. These tribes never attempted to attack any place again, or showed in the open in any large number. Very considerable parties of them took to the Amatola Bush, and in that place and the Water Kloof gave the Imperial forces much trouble in subduing them.

Shortly after this battle all the Imperial forces were withdrawn from the Transkei and the police were kept on a succession of patrols all over Galekaland, the entire force being distributed throughout Kreli's country.

The Galekas were this time thoroughly broken up, and after having been driven three times out of their country, became totally disorganized and distributed amongst other tribes, principally uniting with the Pondoes and Pondomise.

A thousand pounds sterling was offered for Kreli, dead or alive; but he was never captured, though he had several narrow escapes.

The government subsequently withdrew the reward, and this once powerful chief became a wanderer from tribe to tribe, till he surrendered himself as already stated.

A mail service was formed from Ibeka to Toleni, of which I was given charge. With six mules harnessed to a cart I drove between these two places and back twice a week. It was pretty hard work, but was a shade better than constant patrolling. This went on until May, when the mail contractor, seeing the road was safe, resumed the conduct of the mail. I was next sent to King William's Town to be store-keeper for the Colonial Ordnance Department. How I fared and what were my duties I will relate in the next chapter.

CHAPTER 13

Ordnance Department

The Colonial Ordnance Department was not established until after the war had broken out. Before this event, arms and ammunition, and indeed everything, was left to look after itself, in common with all things in the Colonial service.

The officer in charge was a sub-inspector in the police force—one of the very old style of police officers, very uneducated, very obstinate, pig-headed, and ignorant. He hardly knew a Snider rifle from a Martini-Henry; and as for artillery ordnance, he could not distinguish between a shrapnel shell and a case-shot. A brass gun or a steel gun were all the same to him. He was equally ignorant of the charges or projectiles used in the different pieces of ordnance. How could he be expected to know? He had never been taught, had been selected for this post because of his general imbecility, the colonial government thinking that no brains were required to look after ordnance. He certainly fulfilled their expectations in this respect, for a more incompetent person I never had the misfortune to be under. He was always losing something or other.

My first induction into my new position was a request that I would go and try to find a 7-pounder gun, R. M. L., which, with a carriage and limber, altogether weighing about 27 cwt., had been, as he called it, "jumped" by the Imperial authorities. Can the reader imagine anything more absurd? Of what sort could be the machinery of a department, which could lose such a thing as a gun and carriage of this description?

Recollecting the views which had been instilled into me

when I first joined the force, I went down to East London and stopped there a week, and found it a nice change from the Transkei. On my return I walked round King William's Town, and found the "jumped" carriage, together with another that the ordnance storekeeper knew nothing about. After about a month's searching, I at last found the two guns hidden under a quantity of old stores in the police camp.

This is a fair specimen how things were managed in the Colonial Ordnance Department. I soon found out I could do what I liked, and in fact there was very little to do after I had once properly arranged the artillery stores, of which I had charge.

A number of volunteers had to be mounted in King William's Town for service against the Galekas and Gaikas, who had taken refuge in the Amatolas and the surrounding districts. About three miles from King William's Town is the Grand Stand Racecourse. On this course there are tolerably good buildings and ample stabling. These buildings were converted into a hospital for the police who were daily coming down sick from the Transkei, and the stables, with some adjoining paddocks, were used as a depot for the volunteer horses.

An officer of the police was given charge of this re-mount department, as it was termed, and his duty was to buy horses and see them broken in for the service. He had a staff of ten police to help him, and as I knew him well, I requested to be taken on, being heartily sick and tired of the monotony of the ordnance business. I was given charge of the breaking department, and until the termination of hostilities with the Gaikas, did not have a bad time of it by this change.

My chief duties were riding about all day, besides receiving and giving out horses to such corps as required them.

We had to begin early, and generally left off late; but though the work was hard, it was not disagreeable. We had generally between 1000 and 1200 horses to look after, so that it was not all play.

About the end of May I returned to Ibeka and rejoined my troop, the re-mount detachment having been broken up and the horses sold.

Galekaland at this time was quiet, and the patrols were not so frequent.

The government under advice had determined to change the police into a force called the Cape Mounted Rifles. Let me show how this was done. Our commandant, Griffiths, had been promoted to commandant-general. During the period he commanded the police he was far from popular. He was a police officer of the old school. His ideas and sympathies were with the past. He had shown himself in no way mindful of the health or comfort of the force; had worked us very hard, often to no purpose. We were glad to get rid of him, and I dare say he reciprocated the feeling.

Major Moore of the 88th was appointed acting commandant in his place.

The Cape government were contemplating a most unjust, if not an illegal, act towards the men who had joined the police force. If the reader will refer back to the agreement entered into between the Cape agents for the government and the men who were now serving in the police, he will see that in paragraph 2 we had agreed only to serve as police.

The said ------- for the considerations herein after mentioned, hereby agrees and undertakes, &c, &c, to serve the said government as a member of the Cape Frontier Armed and Mounted *Police force,* on the terms and conditions mentioned and contained in the schedule hereto.

Now by an act published in the *Government Gazette* of the Cape of Good Hope of 25th July, 1879, the whole force was changed into the Cape Mounted Rifles, without any previous consultation with the men. We had agreed to serve only as police, and not as soldiers, a point which did not seem in any way to take the attention of the Cape government. Two months previously, with a view to the contemplated change, and as a sop to the officers of the force, they had altered their titles into captains and lieutenants, and thus "squared" them.

They considered it would be a dangerous course to keep the whole force together when carrying out this alteration.

Before the act of parliament was read out to the men they quietly and artfully separated the different troops into as many detachments as possible. This was the first move. The second move was an order, providing that any man who wanted his discharge could have it on application through his commanding officer. As more than two-thirds of the force expressed their desire to be discharged, the order in its effects completely staggered the Cape authorities, who, to get out of it, explained that they proposed this discharge should be limited to the men with bad characters. By this means they consequently secured the discharge of about eighty men, the most useless, discontented, and ill-conditioned in the force, for which no one could possibly blame the Cape government; but is it not evident, that only by ignoring justice altogether could they insist that the men should serve in an entirely new force, without having obtained the previous consent of each individual belonging to the old force? and after issuing an order that all men would be allowed their discharge, if application were made for it, what could justify a departure from the terms or spirit of the order? One consequence immediately arising out of this unjust and impolitic course was, that a whole troop struck in a body, and were marched down to King William's Town.

The men behaved in an orderly manner, but firmly refused to do any duty as Cape Mounted Rifles.

After a good deal of altercation and persuasion, a part of the troop accepted the new position and went to their duty, the remainder were sent to prison as mutinous. There were about 250 prisoners out of a force of 600: many of these men were kept so long in suspense that they got sick of it, and were allowed to return to the ranks, others contrived to desert, and some were imprisoned for various terms.

About this time a number of recruits, forty-five in all, had arrived from England. At home they too had signed to serve in the police, and when they found they were to serve in the C. M. R. they refused duty as well. Fourteen of these men went to prison sooner than serve, eleven deserted, and the remainder were distributed amongst the various troops.

It was much to be regretted that the men did not continue firm in the first attitude they had assumed; the government, it was found, could not dispense with the services of the force. At the same time, the authorities could not have sent 600 men in a body to prison for no fault of their own; in fact, it may be doubted if they would have attempted it. It was wisely resolved to distribute the men about in small detachments, thus preventing the possibility of a meeting amongst the malcontents. Had the Cape government been honest and straightforward enough to state frankly what this new force was to be, these difficulties would hardly have occurred; but they either did not know or would not state what was to be the nature of the conversion of the force. All sorts of rumours were allowed to go forth. All the officers, it was said, were to be discharged, and military officers put in their places. Another report stated that we should be held to serve three years from the date of this conversion, and that our previous time would not be counted. As the Cape government had greatly neglected the force continually, as my narrative has shown, breaking faith with us, the men of course became very dissatisfied and angry.

The Cape Mounted Rifles as a regiment probably now stands second to none in the Imperial service for the work it has to perform; but all the discontented have happily left by the effluxion of time.

But at first a most unwise course was taken. If the government had plainly announced that they intended "to change the F. A. M. Police into Cape Mounted Rifles, giving a higher position to the force, stating the rules under which all will be required to serve, and that the men who do not wish to join the new force can have their discharge," none but the useless and habitual grumblers would have left, and the colonial government would have been saved a great deal of trouble and annoyance. They would also have escaped the scandal of having behaved most dishonourably to a body of men who, having worked and fought hard during the war, deserved far better treatment than they received. If the government, moreover, at this conjuncture had made a clean sweep of all the officers of the police force, and put regular cavalry officers into the new force, they would have made the service extremely popular. But at this time they preferred doing everything with a high hand, and in the most muddle-pated way, with the result I have narrated. As it afterwards turned out, the alterations they made were to extend the period of service from three to five years, to stop two shillings a day in case of sickness instead of the full day's pay, as in the old police force, and last, but not least important, to require men to pass an examination before being promoted to the rank of officers. Such rules were really a strong recommendation to the able men in the force. For what reason the prompt publication of them was not adopted it is difficult to understand.

Major Moore remained but a short time as commandant. He was probably disgusted with the way everything had been conducted. To him succeeded Colonel Bayley. His appointment was most popular with the force, except with one or two of the older officers, who considered they should have succeeded to the command. Fortunately for the colony they did not.

The Cape Mounted Rifles date their birthday as a corps from the appointment of Colonel Bayley. Through his exertions the corps has been brought into the efficient order in which it is at the present time. His first step was to secure the retirement of a good many of the old officers, and promote others from the ranks who had shown special aptitude for the position. I may say more hereafter on the subject of promotions. The way in which of late they have been made has caused much discontent.

The mutineers had all been disposed of, or persuaded into submission, when the depot at Fort Murray again came into life. At this time two non-coms from each troop were ordered to go there, to qualify as drill-instructors for their respective troops.

A sergeant-major and an officer were stationed there. After speaking of this I shall have no further occasion to describe the irregularities suffered in the police force under the old system. Shortly after Colonel Bayley's supervision began, the first thing done was to sweep Fort Murray away with its attendant perquisites and anomalies.

To begin with, the officer in charge of this drill-station

hardly knew his right hand from his left; he was very seldom at the station, and when there was generally more or less inefficient. The sergeant-major had been in the army, but was utterly unsuitable for the post he filled. He was said to have been the mess-sergeant in the same regiment as our previous adjutant. He had no other qualification for the position, as far as I was able to discover. He too was equally inefficient, and the whole of his pupils knew a great deal more about drill and musketry instruction than he did. In fact, after a time, when he discovered this, he used to tell us to drill one another, which we did. Sometimes he would put in an appearance and sometimes not. We none of us learned anything there. The whole thing proved a farce and a waste of time, through the gross ignorance of those who had charge of the station. One day we were all ordered back to our troops, and away we went.

Ibeka was again my destination. This was the last of Fort Murray; it is now let to a farmer. The system pursued there under the police authorities was simple nonsense, neither more nor less.

It was just a nice berth for the adjutant and his pets. It converted good men into bad, and bad into worse. It is now happily a thing of the past, and may be forgotten.

CHAPTER 14
Annexation of St. John's District

On rejoining my troop I found the greater part of my old comrades under orders for St. John's River. The Artillery troop was considerably reduced, numbering at this time not more than sixty men. Of this number thirty were under orders for St. John's. I had never been to St. John's or through any of the surrounding country, further than the Umtata River, so I volunteered to join the party, and was accepted. A few days before we started we heard that Captain Robinson was about to leave, which was a matter of much regret. He did not quit the troop, however, for some four months afterwards, but the day we left Ibeka was the last we saw of him. It was like parting with a dear old friend. We had always pulled well together; he was proud of us, and we were proud of him; he had been with us through all the hardships and privations and dangers we had undergone, sharing them equally with us.

A difference of opinion with the authorities was, I believe, the cause of his resignation. We lost in him a good friend, and the government a tried and valuable officer.

We left Ibeka with our detachment under one officer, one sergeant-major, one sergeant, two corporals, and twenty-eight men; two 7-pounder mountain gun carriages, and twenty days' rations, with ammunition and stores for the guns loaded on two wagons.

The first night we camped at a place called Impuluse, where a trading-station stood. It rained heavily, and we remained here for two days. As soon as the weather cleared we proceeded, and went through Idutywa to the Bashee. We had a considerable difficulty in getting through the river from the stony nature of the drift, and we camped on its banks, remaining there for three days to rest.

The Bashee is a river rising at the foot of the Stormberg, and running in a due easterly direction into the sea, about thirty-three miles from the mouth of the River Umtata. Its volume varies much, according to the rains. The river is nowhere navigable, and has a bad bar at its mouth. The waters are celebrated for eels, the only fish they contain. The country is undulating, with a few trees scattered here and there.

Between the Bashee and the Umtata lies the country of the Tembus, of which Gangeliswe is the chief.

I have already alluded to the character of this friendly chief, and I will in this place give a brief description of his country and people, with a few anecdotes relating to him. Gangeliswe is a tall, well-made, powerful man, above the average height. He invariably dresses in European clothes, and wherever he goes is always accompanied by several of his chiefs and councillors. He is, however, a savage. He has committed some of the most barbarous and brutal murders and acts of cruelty towards his people, such as will not bear repetition in these pages. He is in heart a despicable coward, and generally selects women as objects of his tyranny and oppression.

His great wife was a daughter of Kreli. She was both young and good-looking. Returning one day drunk to his *kraal*, he commenced a row with every one within his reach. He became so violent that his councillors and men about him endeavoured to secure him, and after a time succeeded. He was not long in durance, the men who had secured him thinking that he would be quiet. He made his way to the hut where his wife was, and accused her of having induced these men to tie him up; her denials and remonstrances were in vain; he beat her in the most cruel and brutal manner with his *kerrie* (a stick with a knob at the end), breaking her leg and several of her ribs. She managed to get away, and after a short interval succeeded in reaching her father's *kraal* in Galekaland. Messengers were despatched by Gangeliswe to Kreli, demanding her back. The Galekas requested advice from the Cape government. The reply they obtained told them they could send the woman back or not, as they pleased, but that the government would not support Gangeliswe in his demand, or interfere with the Galekas if they kept her. Happily she was not restored.

Shortly after this another Galeka woman was put to death under circumstances of the most barbarous atrocity. She was murdered by Gangeliswe himself, and Kreli marched his army across the Bashee and attacked the Tembus, who fled, leaving Gangeliswe to take refuge with a missionary. Kreli was persuaded to return to his country by the good offices of the Secretary for native affairs; and Gangeliswe petitioned the government to take his country over, and afford him and his people protection under English laws.

This annexation was effected a few months afterwards, and Gangeliswe was informed, and cautioned to remember that he was now under a government that had the same laws for black and white men; and that if he murdered any one else he would be hanged, or that if he connived at murder he would be severely punished. Since this time he has not openly murdered anyone. Before the annexation of Tembuland, it is known he had murdered five of his wives and several of his children. The people he has caused to be tortured and put to death are numerous. The greater part of his tribe detest him. If he had stayed at home during the Galeka war he would without doubt have been killed by the malcontents of his own tribe.

To avert such an event, which he fully expected, he marched with about 3000 men to Umtata, offered his services to Major Elliot, who accepted them; but as fighting men, they were of little or no use. When the Galekas attacked them they invariably ran.

Some time afterwards, when I had left the service and was farming in Pondoland, I was early one morning in the bush about half a mile from my house, when I found a woman lying under a tree, and apparently dying. I called my native boys, and took her home. After a few days' nursing by an old woman I had on the place she recovered. I then found she too was a wife of Gangeliswe, and that when I discovered her, she was trying to get back to her people, Umditwa's Pondomise. She had been cruelly beaten and stabbed by this fiend in human form, her neck and breast being badly cut. Her back and legs were very much hurt and swollen. I let her remain about the place till she was well, intending to report this occurrence to the magistrate in Umtata; but having to go some little distance one day on business, I found on my return that she had gone away, thus frustrating my intentions in this respect. Some weeks afterwards she sent me two cows, with a message of thanks, and that was the last I heard of her. She was young and not bad-looking. I felt very sorry for her wretched fate, but was glad she had got away safely from her savage lord and master.

The Tembus are a prosperous race, being tolerably rich in cattle, which constitutes a Kaffir's wealth. Their huts are for the most part well built, and their cattle *kraals* are large and commodious. They dress in a mixed costume, half-European, half-native. For instance, you will find some of them wearing trousers, with nothing but a blanket thrown over their shoulders; perhaps another may have the addition of a hat. Many have simply a blanket wrapped round them; but they one and all carry a select assortment of *assegais* and sticks.

The women almost invariably wear a *kaross* and blanket. A *kaross* is a sort of square garment made of several skins sewn together. This is folded round the waist and fastened with a strap or piece of hide over their shoulders. They throw a blanket over their shoulders, and with a gaily-coloured handkerchief round their heads, are considered to be dressed in the height of fashion.

Both men and women daub and smear themselves all over with red clay and grease, and in hot weather the odour is simply horrible.

The men are tall and active, but as a rule have very hard and repulsive faces. The women are not much better. A few of them have regular features and are passable in looks. The most notable quality in a Kaffir woman is her voice. They speak in a soft, subdued manner, and make a very good impression on a first acquaintance. It is not possible, however, for a white man to become much impressed with them on account of their dirt and smell, though intermarriage with them by Europeans is a thing which not unfrequently happens. Let us charitably hope that European husbands make them wash and leave off covering themselves with coloured mud and filth.

The women, from constantly carrying everything, no matter how short the distance, on their heads, have a very upright carriage. They do all the work and labour of the *kraals*. They sow and reap the crops; they fetch water, very often from a long distance; and all the menial work, except milking the cows, is performed by them. The men lie about all day and look on, the small boys and very young men milking the cows and herding the cattle in the day-time.

Polygamy is universally practised amongst these people, the men buying their wives from anywhere they may fancy, and paying cattle for them according to the rank the parents hold in the tribe.

A man may take as many wives as he likes, as long as he can pay the price of them in cattle. The amount varies between six head and thirty head of cattle; but from twelve to fifteen head per wife is the usual average.

The more daughters a father possesses the richer he is considered, and undoubtedly is, for his daughters have a marketable value directly they are of an age to be married, which may be from fourteen to sixteen years.

The way courting is set about is, somewhat peculiar, according to our notions. The intending bridegroom addresses himself to the father of the girl on whom he has set his mind, and says, "I want to make love to your daughter." He then presents him with a small gift. When this preliminary has been gone through, he is allowed to make as much love as he likes to the object of his affections. If a child is the result of this love-making, as it generally is, the man has to pay a fine of one head of cattle to the father. This, however, is taken off the total sum if he ultimately marries the girl. If, on the other hand, he does not marry her, having paid the fine, he is free to go away, and the girl is free to be married to any one. The fact of her having had a child is no detriment to her matrimonial prospects; in fact, if it happens to be a girl, it is regarded as a decided advantage.

The ceremony of marriage varies in different tribes. It generally ends, however, in the same way in every tribe—by all the guests getting very drunk on Kaffir beer, when towards night the most licentious scenes take place, which not unfrequently terminate in bloodshed.

In this tribe also is observed the rite of circumcision, which is practised amongst all the tribes except the Pondos. After the boys attain the age of twelve or thirteen the operation is performed, amidst various dances, and driving of cattle from one place to another; they are then coated over with a white clay, which makes them look as if they had been whitewashed; they are driven away with yells and slight blows from their homes, whence they roam the country round about for three weeks or a month. During this time of excommunication they are allowed to go where they like, steal what they require for food, and commit any enormity that comes into their heads. They may ill-treat women and girls—in fact, do what they like. When they return home they are regarded and take rank as fully grown men and warriors. They no longer milk the cows or herd the cattle, but are admitted to take part in the affairs of their *kraal*. Should they be rich, or can beg, borrow, or steal some cattle, which they generally contrive in some way to do, they take a wife, build a hut, and settle down.

The remarks I have made on the habits and customs of the Tembus apply more or less to all the tribes of South Africa. Ceremonies differ in some tribes, but the customs are the same everywhere, and they always finish up with great drunkenness and excess.

The country from the Bashee River to the Umtata is undulating, with a few trees here and there. It is intersected by a few streams. Towards the coast there are patches of dense bush, containing trees of "yellow wood," which is about the only wood the country produces capable of being sawn into planks. This wood is valuable; a plank of it is worth from five to six shillings.

Bush-cutting, as it is called, is mostly the occupation of

Hottentots, who are all expert sawyers. Occasionally may be found a few white men scattered among them, generally deserters from some of the various regiments which have been stationed in the Cape colony.

Both the Hottentots and the white men work very hard. They live entirely in the bush, and without any of the comforts or privileges of civilized life. They are, as might be expected from the kind of life they lead, an improvident lot. As soon as they have collected a few pounds, they adjourn to the nearest town, and there squander their hard-earned money in drunkenness and riotous dissipation. Bush-cutting is generally the last thing a man adopts. The hard work and "Cape smoke" (spirits) soon make an end of him.

Ten miles from the Bashee, and on the main road, is a precipitous hill called the Emtentu, and here the boundary of the Bomvanas begins. Their chief is Moni, a very old man, and totally blind. His tribe is warlike, and are close friends with the Galekas, whom they materially assisted in the war. Their country extends from the Emtentu to within about eight miles of the Umtata River. It is about twenty-five miles long, and from twenty to thirty miles wide. Several magistrates are resident amongst them, and the tribe is tolerably rich. Horses will not live near the coast, and sheep only in some parts. This tribe also practises polygamy and circumcision, and, in fact, very much resembles the other tribes. The men grow large quantities of tobacco, for which the land is well adapted; but the description is poor, and would be considered hardly worth smoking by the ordinary patron of the fragrant weed. Their huts are covered with grass from the roof to the ground. In this they differ from other tribes, who only thatch the tops, and plaster with mud the remainder of the walls.

In due time, and without adventure of a notable kind, we reached Umtata, and camped close to the river, not sorry for a rest, which we were to have for a week before proceeding to St. John's River, of the road to which place we had heard the most fearful accounts.

CHAPTER 15

Tembuland

The Umtata River rises at a junction of the Quambi and Umbolapo Hills, about twenty miles in a northerly direction from the city of Umtata, which is situated about twenty-five miles from the eastern coast. The town of Umtata is built on the Tembu side of the river, and is the seat of the chief magistrate of Tembuland. There is also a resident magistrate in the city.

Nearly all the houses and stores are built of galvanized iron sheeting, the cathedral being erected of the same material. There are about a hundred houses of different sizes and shapes intermixed with large Kaffir huts.

The town has sprung up entirely in the last five years; as lately as 1875 there were only three houses in the locality. In addition to the cathedral there is a Wesleyan chapel of brick, and a courthouse built of stone.

The population of white men, including the surrounding farmers, with the inhabitants of the town, is about 400; but the country is rapidly filling up, the climate being most favourable to farming and stock-raising. Sheep, horses, and ostriches do well.

Umtata is one of the few places where there is little or no horse sickness. The white inhabitants are nearly all English, or descended from English parents. The rest are Dutch, but they are a very small minority, and much disliked.

In Umtata, to call a man a Dutchman is regarded as the greatest insult you can give. The people pride themselves on being English and having English ways. Before the present Basuto war there was always a strong body of police stationed at this place. Umtata is literally surrounded by Kaffirs on all sides. Tembus, Bomvanas, Halas, are on one side, and on the other Pondos and Pondomise. In case of any of these tribes breaking into rebellion, a strong force would be necessary to hold the place from invasion. It has lately been the scene of much trouble and bloodshed, but at the time we passed through it the natives were all quiet. I am describing the condition of affairs in October, 1878. The weather was beginning to be very hot. There is no forest, nor are there any trees within ten miles of the town. The country is flat on the Tembu side, and on the Pondo side there are rolling valleys.

The district is liable to severe storms at certain seasons of the year, and we had reached the time when these disturbances generally occur. One afternoon in particular, the weather was unusually hot; thunder had been heard continually in the distance since mid-day; those who understood the signs prophesied a violent storm. About three o'clock small whirlwinds of dust were seen coming down the roads. A cold chilling breeze followed, several very vivid flashes of lightning succeeded with heavy claps of thunder. Immediately down came the rain, in what I can only call buckets-full, the lightning and thunder continuing without intermission. When the rain ceased the wind blew, and with so much violence that it unroofed several houses. Our tents of course were completely blown down, and some carried away several yards. Everything was wet through. About an hour after this violent conflict of the elements, all ceased, everything became again tranquil, and it was deliciously cool.

These sort of storms of more or less violence occur three or four times a week at Umtata during the summer months. I lived to experience many more subsequently to the one I have described, and to see the entire roof of the Bishop's house blown a distance of a hundred and fifty yards, but this was in a storm of exceptional violence.

The mission here, of which Bishop Callaway is the head, has not been established a sufficient time to manifest any improvement in the adjoining territory, but in the town of Umtata itself, a great deal of good has unquestionably been effected. Before the arrival of the Bishop, the place was notorious as being the most lawless in the colony. It was the haunt of outlaws and blackguards of every description, and of all colours, who made it their headquarters. Magistrates and a better class of people have changed all this, and it is now a flourishing, well-to-do English town.

We heard very discouraging accounts of the road to St. John's River. Our commanding officer was advised to hire two more wagons, and to divide the loads; but he declined, I suppose being incredulous of the reports he had heard. To our cost we found that report had in no way been exaggerated. After a week's rest to recruit the strength of our horses and bullocks, we began our troubles, leaving Umtata early in the morning, and making no more than about ten miles that day. The roads during our first three days were tolerable in comparison with what we afterwards found; but we had occasionally to hook one span of oxen in front of another, and so pull over the hills, as far as a place called Bunting. We contrived to get over the ground pretty well so far, but the struggle was to come.

All the country through which we had passed presented to the eye scenery of the most beautiful description, plenty of trees and water, with an abundance of grass. It was the country of Umquiliso, the recognized or paramount chief of the Pondos.

It fell to my lot afterwards to have a good deal of intercourse with this chief and his people; so I may be allowed to say something of them and their ways. Pondoland is divided into two parts, over which there are two ruling chiefs, Umquiliso and Umquiquela. Umquiliso's country lies between the Umtata and the St. John's River; he has several inferior chiefs subject to him. The principal ones are Xombella, Gwadiso, Nangewa, and Valala. Xombella is Umquiliso's brother. The whole of his tribe number about 20,000 men. They are a lazy race and rich. Well-formed, fine-looking men, greatly superior to the ordinary Kaffirs, but they are, at the same time, arrant cowards. Their cattle are famous throughout the whole colony, and are much sought after. They make superior *trek* oxen, and are equally advantageous for the butcher. These oxen greatly exceed in height and bulk any of our most prized breeds in England.

Umquiliso and Umquiquela are the sons of a former chief, Damas, who was always very anxious to keep on friendly terms with the English. He encouraged traders into his country, affording them many advantages, and always extended to them abundant protection. Umquiliso had followed in his father's footsteps; but his brother Umquiquela only partly so. For a long time Umquiquela has been suspected of inviting his people to make war against the English. He had been accused also a long time past of inciting quarrels between his own people and the M'quesibes, a tribe to the north under a chief called Jo-jo, and who is under British protection. All this he has done simply with a view to provoke a war, if possible, with the white man.

The country of which Umquiquela is chief extends from St. John's River N.E. to the Umzimkulu. At this time the territory in question had been declared by the English forfeited to Umquiliso, who thus became paramount chief of the whole tribe. But the English declaration to this effect does not seem to have availed much, the Pondos still adhering to their former chiefs. A resident magistrate is located close to Umquiquela, the only change which has been effected under the English declaration.

The two brothers have been at loggerheads for years, and much good could not be anticipated unless they had been reconciled.

Umquiquela is an old man, nearly always drunk; and Umquiliso is too lazy to see any one except his wives and friends.

The Cape government at this time had just completed the purchase from Umquiliso of a strip of country extending about eight miles from the mouth of the River St. John, and about a mile broad. Umquiquela, as the elder brother and the hitherto recognized head of the Pondos, expostulated, to no purpose. He strenuously urged that Umquiliso had no right to sell it. This protest apparently made no difference. The government had no difficulty in persuading Umquiliso to take the money and give them a title to the district, which we may be sure they have no intention to relinquish.

The object of our proceeding at this time to St. John's, was to take possession for the government of this strip of land. A company of the 24th Regiment was at the same time despatched

114

from Natal. These proceedings in the matter did not tend to improve the feelings between the brothers, more particularly as Umquiliso, though younger, had changed places with his brother as paramount chief. It was with a view to prevent or settle any disturbances which might arise between these chiefs and their people the government were now stationing a force in this newly-acquired district. Having something more to say about Umquiliso, his country, and people, I defer my remarks to the close of these pages, that I may take the reader through the remainder of our journey to St. John's River.

At Bunting we encamped for a week, that the cattle, as well as the men, might be thoroughly rested before proceeding further. We no longer required information at this point respecting the character of the roads. The appearance of the country was quite sufficient to indicate what work was before us. Not a single piece of level ground could be seen as far as the eye could reach; nothing but numerous and precipitous hills appeared, some of them very high, all rugged and steep on every side; many rivers running between them, and abundant bush. Through this country we were about to travel. Except by the immediate settlers round Umtata, and the traders in Pondoland, the country was very little known. The road, if entitled to such a description, was bad beyond all conception—so bad that the greatest difficulty is experienced to persuade owners of wagons to "ride the road," as it is there called. We could find, in fact, only two men who would lend any help; but they had spans of magnificent oxen, which were used to the road. These two drivers would not put more than 4,000 pounds weight on each wagon, or about 36 cwt, the general load on ordinary roads being between 9,000 and 10,000 pounds weight, to be drawn in either case by about sixteen oxen. The owners charged, of course, what they liked. Our own spans of oxen were pretty good, but they were not accustomed to such inaccessible hills; and when we had contrived to start, we proceeded but slowly and with great difficulty.

Bunting is distant thirty-three miles from Umtata, and twenty-eight from St. John's River. A mission-station was formerly at this place, but it is now removed nearer Umtata.

It was the first mission in Pondoland, and a very old one. It was established, I understood, about 1822. There is, however, a trading-station about a mile distant from Bunting, in a beautiful valley, at a large farm-house owned by a Mr. Berry, who is an Irishman, and has been settled there several years. He has a large family, and is very rich. We found him a most hospitable, kind old gentleman; and I shall always remember him for the considerate way he invariably received and entertained us whenever we had occasion to visit his house, which, in the discharge of our duties, we frequently did.

Early one morning we started from Bunting, not without many misgivings. After travelling for about three miles along a tolerably rough road, but up to this time not very hilly, we reached a hill called the Quanyana, descending at an angle of about fifty degrees. The hill is about three-quarters of a mile long, and perfectly straight. It was here our real troubles began. The first wagon, owing to the steepness of the descent, went down at a terrific pace, the frightened oxen galloping as hard as they were able. About half way down the wagon, as was to be expected, turned completely over, scattering everything all over the place. The horses were all sent down to the bottom of the hill in charge of a third of our party, off-saddled, and turned loose to graze; the remainder of us then set to work to right the wagon and reload it. This occupied us three good hours of very hard work. But this misadventure was as nothing compared with what was to come. We cut down small trees and hung them behind this reloaded wagon as a drag, and eventually we reached the bottom in safety, and outspanned. We had now gained a little experience, and hanging trees behind the second wagon, this came down in safety, and was also *out-spanned*. From the bottom of this hill a road runs for about three miles tolerably level to the foot of another hill, to which, after a short rest, we proceeded, and again outspanned, this time for the night.

This hill in front, which we came to ascend in the morning, is half a mile long, and has a gradient of about sixty degrees. At daylight we started. Very soon it became apparent that the wagons were not going up with the loads they had on them. After

116

vainly howling at the oxen and belabouring the poor things for some time, nothing remained but to take off half the load. This we did, with a great deal of labour and trouble; but even then, with no more than 2,500 pounds weight on, the oxen could not pull the load forward. There was nothing for it but to hook the other span on, one in front of the other: so with thirty-six oxen for our team, we managed to get along. Arriving at the top of the hill, we had to off load, and bring the empty wagon down for the remainder; and then when once more we had reached the top, to load the remainder on. Had there been but one wagon this hindrance would have been serious enough; but when the whole of the process I have described had to be repeated with the second wagon, it came to be not only a hindrance, but exceedingly tiresome and hard work.

Let me bring to a conclusion the description of this most arduous journey. We had come on the top of this hill, to the last piece of flat ground we experienced. For the rest of the way it was nothing but up and down, from this time till we reached St. John's. Some of the hills were over a mile long, and always steep; the last hill we had to ascend we literally scrambled up—I can call it by no other name. We occupied two whole days in reaching the top, only to find another hill just as long to go down. We used to load and unload several times a day. Not unfrequently one of the wagons would capsize, and half the contents roll about in every direction, only to be saved by carrying the things up by hand with great labour and fatigue.

When we at last reached St. John's River, eight of our oxen had died, and all the men were more or less ill. Two of our comrades, indeed, died shortly afterwards, and were buried on the banks of the river, far away, poor fellows, from home and friends. The horses fared the best. We had never travelled more than four miles a day, and some days could accomplish no more than a mile. Seventeen days were occupied from Bunting to the river, the distance being no more than twenty-eight miles, our average rate of progress being about one and three-quarter miles a day.

But we were well rewarded for our long and difficult journey. The scenery was grand—beautiful mountains covered with bush and trees. Between the mountains flowed the St. John's River, called by the natives the Umzinvubu—a splendid expanse of flowing water, at the place we camped, about 300 yards wide. We wanted a good rest previous to building a permanent camp, as we understood we should remain here some time. As I spent some months in this place not altogether in an unpleasant way, I will devote my next chapter to a description of the country and the surroundings of this beautiful spot. In various ways it proved full of interest. South Africa cannot boast of a more glorious or a more promising situation.

CHAPTER 16

St. John's River and District

The Umzinvubu, or St. John's River, rises at a place called Speken Kop, on the borders of Basutoland, and runs in a southeasterly direction into the sea. It is navigable for about nine miles from the mouth for vessels of tolerably light draft, There is plenty of water inside the river, but a shifting bar, which is common to all South African rivers, makes the entrance difficult, and at times dangerous. On this bar there are varying depths, sometimes as much as eighteen feet at high water Spring tides. The average depth at high water may be taken at nine feet; and it never falls below six feet, and is often much higher than the first-mentioned figure, nine feet. The depth varies much, according to the strength and duration of the freshets coming down the river, and is ruled also in some degree by the prevalence of easterly or westerly winds. Small steamers regularly run to St. John's from Port D'Urban, and have no difficulty in entering or leaving the river. There is a harbour-master, and a staff of boatmen and pilots, who keep the bar and river well buoyed. There is also a custom-house with landing, and a bonded warehouse with the usual staff of officers. These establishments have been made since the district was purchased by the Cape government. Umzinvubu means in Kaffir the river of the seahorse or hippopotamus, of which there are many in the river. They present strange sights swimming up and down, landing only at night, making great havoc in the *mealie* (Indian corn) gardens. A few are shot every year, but it does not appear to make any difference in the number of them. During the time I was at St. John's they certainly increased. One night, about the commencement of the Zulu war, we were all turned out by a sentry of the 24th, who declared that he saw natives making towards the fort. Upon investigation the supposed enemy turned out to be a number of these beasts, which were playing about on the mud and sand on the river bank. A shot soon dispersed them; but as it was not positively discovered what had caused the alarm till nearly daylight, we were kept under arms all night through their eccentricities, and you may be sure we did not particularly bless them for thus disturbing our rest.

After a few days quiet, both the soldiers and the C. M. R. set to work to build a fort and a camp. The fort was built by the detachment of soldiers, and constructed in the form of a square, with houses all round the quadrangle inside. A large and deep ditch was excavated on the outside, and two bastions for the guns were placed at the corners. This fort we built on the top of a small hill and in an excellent position, commanding a drift or ford at the highest navigable point on the river.

The C. M. R. camp was placed about 500 yards from the fort, and was also built in the form of a square. We employed some natives on hire to build some of the huts, and we constructed the stables ourselves. A deep ditch was also excavated for our protection, and a thick wattle fence enclosed the camp all round. This completed our arrangement. Four men were told off for the occupation of each hut, and we were all very comfortable.

We were occupied, however, seven months on these buildings, but the time was well spent, as was evident when the whole was finished. Standing on a good position, and on a slightly rising ground, we had made an excellent shelter; and had we been attacked, should have given a very good account of our invaders.

Though rumours of all sorts continually reached us that an attack was imminent, we were not molested. A very definite report was brought that the Pondos of Umquiquela would attack us, and we indeed received a message from that chief to the effect that unless we withdrew from the country he would drive us into the sea. Nothing came of these indications or threats, and we passed a quiet time during the whole period I was stationed there, which was not altogether unwelcome. Discipline came to be much relaxed. We confined ourselves to evening parades and a drill once in a week. Our horses nearly all unfortunately died from horse sickness. We had literally little or nothing to do, and this at times made even our well-earned rest somewhat irksome. For recreation we bought a boat from one of the steamers, and passed some of our time in fishing and shooting on the river, with various success.

Nothing of importance occurred except on one occasion, which I must not omit to relate. Some five months after our arrival a non-commissioned officer, accompanied by a private, was sent into Umtata to bring money to St. John's to pay the men. On their return, as they came near the encampment, they were stopped by a couple of natives, who seized their bridles, and commenced chattering in Kaffir, which one of them could not understand at all, and the other very little. The non-commissioned officer was struck violently on the arm with a heavy stick, and saw at once that the intention of these men was to rob them of the money they had in charge, over £400, and that they had evidently waylaid them for this purpose; so he drew his revolver and shot one man through the chest; the other native immediately ran away. On their arrival at St. John's in safety they reported the occurrence to the commanding officer, and here the matter dropped, as we supposed. But it was not the end of it, as I will show.

On the banks of the St. John's River is a large store belonging to Messrs. White Brothers.[1] They have been in this store for several years, and have made a good deal of money, especially before the advent of competition and Custom-House restrictions.

The river in earlier times afforded excellent opportunities for smuggling guns and ammunition for sale and barter with the natives; and this special trade was extensively carried on in this river without a doubt. Even now, in a less degree, the same

---

1. This is the firm whose manager, Mr. Campell, refused in July 1881 to pay duty on a cargo of goods consigned to them from Natal, settling the question at the time by a number of Pondos rushing on board the vessel, tying the captain to the mast and forcibly carrying the goods on shore in spite of the protestations of the Sub-collector of customs. See *Standard*, July 21st, 1881.

trade is followed; but the river having come into the hands of the Cape government, as I have explained, this business, which is contraband, has been very seriously affected.

One of the members of Messrs. White's firm resided at the store I have mentioned. When the force first arrived we found ourselves short of provisions, and Messrs. White at once doubled the price of everything. We regarded his conduct as indefensible. The men wished to purchase his fowls, of which he had hundreds; but he would not sell to us. We thought not so much of this, there being in the river quantities of geese swimming about, but they very soon disappeared; what became of them I leave the reader to conjecture.

This White was in the habit of holding a service in Kaffir in a sort of chapel he had built; in fact, he had turned himself into a missionary, praying on Sunday with the Kaffirs, and exhorting them to come to his store on week days, where they were safe to be swindled. In the goodness of his heart he no doubt thought it a great sin that a C. M. R. should shoot one of his black brethren, though the black brother had attempted to commit highway robber)'. Anyway, he made some very officious remarks, and busied himself in a most uncalled-for way respecting the incident to which I have alluded. Speaking Kaffir as well as a native, he interposed on behalf of the native who had been shot, determined, if possible, to get the force into a scrape. The man who had been shot, it seems, was not mortally wounded. He had the bullet extracted; and conscious of having been in the wrong, he refrained from reporting to his chief, Umquiliso, what had happened; and as he failed in his attempt to steal the money, he kept quiet and held his tongue. Five months afterwards this occurrence was communicated to Umquiliso, who at first would not believe that any such thing had happened, the injured man having made no report to him. He only remarked, "Why has not the injured man been to me, his chief!"

After a time he was induced to make a representation to the chief magistrate at Umtata, and requested that the matter might be investigated. The non-commissioned officer and private of the C. M. R. were accordingly sent under escort to Umtata, and after being detained in arrest for some short time, were tried and fined.

This course was taken to keep friends with the Pondos and the two riflemen were put through the form of being punished so as not to raise any questions of difficulty with the Pondos. The men's prospects in the force were not prejudiced by the proceedings, for both of them were promoted shortly after their release. The officiousness of this trading missionary nearly involved the Cape government in very serious consequences. The anger of the men against White knew no bounds. He soon after the trial "fell off" the jetty and was seriously hurt. The men regarded it as a judgment, and no one would have cared had he broken his neck. It is this stamp of men that do such infinite harm in the colony, taking the part of the natives in everything, right or wrong. By their stupid, inconsiderate behaviour they eventually teach the Kaffirs to believe that what they do is right, and what the white men do is wrong. Perpetual misunderstandings are the result, and the natives imagine that the whites are imposing on them, when, as a rule, they are simply proposing what is for their benefit.

The river runs towards the sea through two high hills, called the Gates of St. John's. These hills are covered with bushes. The trees rise from the edge right up to the top, and the acclivity is nearly perpendicular. On the east side of the river the bank is 350 feet high, and on the west it is over 400 feet. Vast quantities of monkeys, baboons, and parrots are found in this bush. They chatter and scream at you all the way down the river. A boat was at this time the quickest means of going from the fort to the mouth. The road was little more than an indifferent footpath, going a long way round, the banks of the river being quite impracticable. A good road has since been constructed all the way down suitable for wagons, and the Cape government is spending large sums of money, improving both the harbour and the communication with Umtata; but some time must elapse before these important works can be completed.

Being of Cornish extraction, and understanding a little about geology and minerals, I spent a part of my spare time in investigating and prospecting the strata. I made sundry experiments with small sieves, washing the soil in various places, and I found "value" in the beds of the numerous small streams flowing into the St. Johns. The results I obtained from these trials may not be uninteresting to our readers.

The rocks in the two hills we have described as the *gates* are stratified and almost perpendicular, having a slight inclination only towards the N.-E. and S.-E. The gap through which the river flows is evidently the result of erosion from a very remote period. On both sides of the river the strata are the same, and are reposing on granite, which is seen cropping out at the distance of about half-a-mile from the river. Some clay-slate interposes before the junction. The whole disposition of the rocks seemed very much to resemble the junction of the Silurian system with the clay-slate and granite as I have seen them on the north-east coast of Cornwall, except that a red stone in the several members of the Silurian strata took the place of the blue *elvans* and other rocks.

About four miles from the mouth of the river, immediately above the *gates*, the land becomes flat and somewhat undulating. As there were no excavations of any kind, I had no opportunity of examining the rocks below. Above the fort, however, at no great distance there is another perpendicular hill opened out in the same way as the *gates*, the work, no doubt, of the river. On one side at this point is a deep bed of whitish sand. The surface on the top is of clay, and below is a sort of trap rock, then clay-slate and granite. The dip of all this is to the south, and the granite is in a transition state, and showed strong symptoms of copper, traces of which I found in it, but to no great extent.

My favourite haunts were higher up the river. On the slopes of the hills the granite cropped out in several places, and at the junction of the hills at the bottom of their slopes ran several small streams. I contrived several rough sieves, and placed them at various parts of these rivulets. In a week's time I obtained altogether, by the simple washing down of the river, nearly two ounces of gold, with no labour except carrying the sieves to the selected places. I also tested several spades full of soil taken up indiscriminately from the deposits of these streams, and I invariably found gold in them, but in small quantities.

About four miles away from the fort and from the mouth of the river was a curious fissure, into which I managed to get one day when strolling about, and had great difficulty in getting out of it. At the time I discovered the fissure it was filled with underwood, through which I fell some ten feet or more. So struck was I with the look of the place, that I determined to give it a good overhauling in a day or two. One morning, accompanied by my chum and a native boy carrying food and kettles, we set off and began work. The layers of strata were perpendicular and covered nearly all over with moss, but after knocking this off with a pick, together with the external soil, we came upon some likely-looking ground for copper. In about two hours' time, after working all the time, we had breakfast, and then began work again. After driving in with the pick about a yard and a half, I saw that we were getting away from the lode, if lode there was, and that we must either look for it much lower down on the same side, or, going to surface, try the other side of this fissure. I *dialed* the line of the lode with a pocket compass as well as I could, and this made us resolve to start on the other side of the fissure. I regret to say that at this period of our day's work we had dinner, and having lit our pipes, afterwards went sound asleep, and remained so until the black boy awoke us. He wanted to know if we intended sleeping there all night in the bush.

As we had to be back for evening parade we started at once, leaving our tools hidden in the under-wood. For some few days after this it rained hard, and one thing and another turning up, I was unable to visit my spot for nearly a month. One morning the same man and I started off again, my companion bringing his gun with him this time, as he declared he had had enough mining to last him his life. I pitched upon the spot where I thought I should cut across the lode, and after working hard for an hour, I came on some *mundic* and the same-looking soil as on the opposite side of the fissure. I still thought I was too low, so I went to where some granite was cropping up, and as I had been working in slate, I knew I could not be far from the junction. After some two hours' more labour, during which time my friend came back with a splendid bush buck, telling me I was mad to go on, I struck on a lode of virgin copper. I brought away a good many lumps of ore, and afterwards had them assayed in the colony. One lump contained 65% of copper and another about 42%.

This was all the mining I was able to do, being shortly afterwards called to Ibeka. I was never subsequently able to visit the place. The lode I hit was about eleven inches wide where I cut into it, and immediately on the junction of the granite and slate. The copper here could, without doubt, be profitably worked. The place where I found it is close to the river, and a waterfall is near, which could easily be made available for machine power. Shipping anything from St. John's River has become an easy matter, and I venture to prophesy, that at no very distant period minerals will be extensively worked and exported from this river.

There are several more lodes further away, and further still up the country, towards Dordrecht, are extensive coal-fields. These now are being worked to advantage. A practical miner would soon discover the minerals. Several known lodes exist all over the immediate country. I have seen many other places with copper cropping out of the ground; but the one I have just described is by far the richest, and at the same time would be most easily worked. Should any of my readers feel interested in what I have stated, and wish to know more of the matter, I shall be pleased to give any further information in my power.

CHAPTER 17

Failure at Morosi's Mountain

Having now returned to Ibeka, I will proceed to notice the events which had happened in Basutoland since the beginning of the year 1879.

In the south-west corner of Basutoland dwelt a Basuto chieftain named Morosi. His tribe are called Baphutis. He had several sons, one of whom was named Dodo. Morosi's strip of country had been given him by Moshesh, the chief of the Basutos, some years previously, in return for services rendered during several wars with neighbouring tribes, and more particularly during the comparatively recent war with the Orange Free State.

Old Morosi had been a famous general in days gone by. He had commanded an army which had been mainly instrumental in defeating Sir George Cathcart, when he attacked the Basutos in 1853. Here he was reaping the reward of his service, living on this strip of land, when he was brought into trouble through his sons—trouble which terminated in the death of himself and the greater part of his tribe, and the scattering of all who were left. At the beginning of the year, in common with the Basutos, of whom he and his people formed a part, he was under the protection of the Cape government. The resident magistrate with Morosi, a Mr. Austin,[1] lived at a place called Silver Spruit. One of Mr. Austin's duties was to collect hut-tax from these people at various times. He had no white force nearer than Palmetfontein, twenty-five miles distant, where a troop of C. M. R. were stationed. About a dozen black policemen were at his disposal at his residence.

---

1. Killed during the last Basuto war.

For a long time Dodo had been stirring up the Baphutis to refuse to pay these hut-taxes, which, when the country had been taken over by the government, these natives, through their chiefs, had agreed to pay.

This disagreement, which had been going on for some time, at last culminated in a flat refusal to pay any sum to the collector. Mr. Austin had no alternative but to summon the offenders, and having duly warned them, he committed them to prison until the tax was paid.

Dodo, who was present when the committal of these men took place, threatened Mr. Austin with personal violence, and declared he would release the prisoners. An attempt was made to arrest him, but without success. He was the son of a great chief, and I have no doubt the black policemen felt compunction in doing their duty as they ought to have done, more particularly being Baphutis themselves. Mr. Austin duly reported this state of things to the Cape government, and requested that some force might be sent to support his authority. Fifty men of the C. M. R. were accordingly moved up to a place called Stork Spruit; but whilst on the march, before they had time to arrive, Dodo and a strong party of Baphutis broke open the gaol and released the prisoners. Mr. Austin pluckily stuck to his post, sent to Morosi to deliver up Dodo and the remainder of the ring-leaders, and at last went personally to Morosi, and represented to him to what consequences a refusal to do this would certainly lead. Either Morosi could not or would not make them surrender; but, any way, he did not exert himself in the matter, or render any information or help to the government.

Mr. Austin, whose life was in considerable danger, retired to Stork Spruit, and the Baphutis immediately wrecked the residency and buildings.

No. 4 troop were marched into Morosi's country and had a brush with the rebels, losing three men and killing a few of the natives.

Morosi first of all took possession of a mountain close to Stork Spruit, and here for several days defied all attempts to dispossess him or disperse his people. The whole of the Baphutis probably numbered no more than 1500 men, with the usual quantity of women and children. The Cape government still wanted to give him a chance, and offered to let him go back to his own country with his people, if he would deliver up Dodo and the remainder of the men who had broken into the gaol. Morosi requested to be allowed a week for consideration; during the interval he gradually removed the whole of his tribe, with their cattle and horses, to another mountain, some twenty miles distant, from which he never came down alive. So artfully was this done, that no one knew anything about it until the time arrived for his answer, when it was discovered that only a few women remained behind. These, of course, knew nothing, or if they did, would tell nothing. They were released a few hours afterwards, and probably rejoined their friends, rejoicing at their easy escape. The Cape government were now involved in what promised to be a very nice little war. The country was extremely difficult of access. There were literally no roads, grass was scarce, and the mountain on which Morosi had taken refuge was known to be in a very strong natural position, which had been strengthened by well-built fortifications. For the last ten years Morosi had made the fortification of this place his hobby. He had been crazy on the subject of having a fortified mountain. He had spent his energy, and ten good years of his life, on this work, and certainly he had succeeded in making the place almost impregnable. He had plenty of ammunition, food, and cattle on the top of the mountain, with several houses and huts, and he was well able to resist a long siege, and he knew it as well as any one. I will here briefly describe this mountain, which was to cost much to the colony in life and money before it was finally taken.

Morosi's Mountain stands at an elbow of the Orange River. On three sides it is perfectly perpendicular. The fourth side is a slope of about a mile and subtending an angle of about thirty degrees. This slope was protected with a series of *schanzes* or walls, about eight to twelve feet high, loopholed for rifles and guns, and very strongly built. Artillery against the walls was utterly useless; the shell might knock a stone or two away, but nothing approaching a gap would be produced. About nine of these walls were placed at different intervals up this slope. The walls were built right across, and if you got over one, it was only to be stopped by another just in front of you, and so on right up to the top. The top of this mountain was about a mile long and about half a mile broad, and was also completely *schanzed* in every direction. Cross *schanzes* were built in between those running across, so that wherever you went, or wherever you tried to get over one of these walls, you were met by cross firing in three or four directions.

Such is a very rough-and-ready description of a place which somehow or other we had to take. I have described it as it was after we had captured it. Before it was taken, it was certain death to go within 500 yards of the first *schanze*. The Baphutis are splendid shots, and they kept all their fortifications constantly manned. About 1200 yards from the first *schanze*, and running at right angles to it, towards the east, was a narrow neck of stone terminating in a small hill, which was called by us the Saddle; the whole length of this neck and hill was about 700 yards. On the north side of this the Orange River turned sharp round past the larger mountain, and flowed towards the N.-E., being joined some few hundred yards farther away by a tributary stream named the Quithing. On the Quithing side was a large fissure in the perpendicular rock, called afterwards Bourne's Crack. There were in this crack huge natural steps, about twenty or thirty feet apart, surmounted at the top by a large overhanging rock.

Across the fissure I have described at the top was a distance of about six feet, and from the summit of the over-hanging rock to what I may call the first step was about twenty feet. From the top to the bottom of this precipice was a distance of about seventy feet.

It is necessary to trouble the reader with these minute details, for it was up this last place the mountain was eventually taken. When Morosi had first placed himself in this stronghold, three troops of the C. M. R. had been sent up, and an attempt was made to surround the mountain, and as far as possible prevent any communication between Morosi and the outside world. These three troops of C. M. R mustered no more than 250 men, and were utterly inadequate to cover the ground which had to be secured, to effectually prevent any communication. The Cape government had just formed three colonial regiments of a force entitled yeomanry. The enrolment of this corps had been the subject of much adverse criticism, and the premier, to show what the were made of, called the greater part of them out, and ordered them up to Morosi's Mountain. He belauded these men to the skies on their departure from their various head-quarters, making some very unjust and disparaging remarks about the C. M. R., which corps at the rime in question, under the ne formation and discipline, had only been in existence little over six months. The yeomanry were to take this mountain out of hand, and for all the good the C. M. R. were, they might just as well be away The premier had not, however, the same opinion the artillery, for he ordered up the whole troop with three guns, purchased a 12-pounder Whitworth, a steel rifled gun, from the Orange Free State, with plenty of ammunition for it, and did not call out any of the volunteer artillery.

The first organized attack took place in May, when the whole force, under one of the colonels of these redoubtable yeomanry regiments, assaulted the mountain, and were thoroughly beaten off by the Baphutis, losing over twenty men killed and wounded in the attack. The attacking party never got within 100 yards of the first *schanze*; and the loss to the enemy afterwards turned out to be nil. The yeomanry individually were good men, but they were not organized, and were much worse in point of discipline than the old F. A. M. Police in its worst days. They were also, with few exceptions, badly led.

The next attack was to take place in July, the troops in the meantime being reinforced by burghers, a contingent of Hottentots, and another troop of C. M. R. The day before the attack a sergeant of artillery[2] and seven men volunteered to creep up at night and throw in shell with lighted fuses over the *schanzes* to drive the enemy's sharpshooters out, and enable the storming-party to get over the *schanzes*. They were to creep up at night, and then lie under the *schanzes* until the storming-party was

---

2. Sergeant Scott.

ready to advance. They all succeeded in getting up safely, and lay down right underneath the wall, waiting for daylight. The attack this time was to be made under the direction of the gallant Griffiths, our late commandant, and now commandant-general, and he made as great a mess of this as he had of our movements in the Galeka war. He was ably assisted in this mess-making by the greater part of the yeomanry and burghers.

The C. M. R. were to advance, and the burghers and yeomanry to support them; in the meantime, the *schanzes* were to be cleared by the shell party lying underneath. The advance was sounded, Sergeant Scott and his party threw two shells over the *schanze*, the third burst in his hand, shattering it and severely wounding him and three others of the party. The C. M. R. charged and got possession of the first *schanze*, shooting a few of the enemy; but with the exception of a few of the yeomanry and burghers, who gallantly supported them, the rest of these boasted corps could not be induced to advance up the hill. One of the colonels I saw in a hole under a stone shouting to his men to go on, but not venturing his own valuable person out of cover. This was the same gentleman who had, some two years before, accused the police of running away at Guadana. I hope if he ever reads these pages he will be pleased with the notice I have taken of him.

The grand result of this ill-judged and mismanaged attack was our most ignominious defeat. We lost heavily in killed and wounded. Captain Surmon of the CM. R. was shot through the lungs, and about thirty-four were killed and wounded on our side, with an insignificant loss to the enemy. Such was the result of the day's proceedings.

Sergeant Scott had his hand amputated. I am glad to say he has since been promoted and received the V. C.; but he was for a long time dangerously ill from his wounds.

Winter was now coming on; it was bitterly cold, with hard frosts at night. The Baphutis, finding they had beaten us off, used to make frequent sorties against the camp; but our camp was too well guarded for them to surprise us. One of the yeomanry camps, however, at the junction of the Quithing and

Orange Rivers, was surprised one night, and seventeen men killed on the spot. After this last episode we had no more surprises in the camp.

A party of our men went up one night to reconnoitre the *schanzes*, were surprised, and one of them wounded and taken prisoner. The next morning his head appeared on a pole shown over the *schanze* on the top of the mountain; his body was flung over a few hours afterwards, which we recovered and buried. Let us hope, poor fellow, his tortures were but brief; but we remembered this against the Baphutis when we afterwards took the mountain.

Our horses were now daily dying, and the whole force getting sick. It was with great difficulty that provisions had been supplied us; but up to this time the commissariat arrangements had been good. The supply of forage for the horses now failed, and there being little or no grass, the poor beasts, between hunger and cold, rapidly died off. The authorities at last determined to wait till the weather was a little warmer and also to try and starve the enemy out by surrounding the mountain. They of course did not know the stores of food on the top, and the means by which the enemy were almost daily supplied, and which was not found out until after the mountain was captured.

The best part of the force now assembled was ordered away, leaving just sufficient to surround the mountain. These consisted of an equal number C. M. R., yeomanry, and burghers, with a few native levies, principally Fingoes. The artillery were ordered to Ibeka to refit, leaving two guns and detachments with an officer in charge. The remainder of us marched to Ibeka on foot in twenty-three days, heartily glad of a rest and change, which, however, was not to be of long duration.

CHAPTER 18

Capture of Morosi's Mountain

The beginning of October again found us on the way to Morosi's Mountain. Since our return to Ibeka the guns and carriages had been refitted, and all of us been provided with fresh horses and equipments.

Our road lay through Fingoland, and until arrived at Queenstown, was of a most uninteresting description. Seven days after leaving Ibeka we reached Queenstown, a pretty and prospering town to the north border of Fingoland, in the district bearing the same name. Queenstown was originally built in the form of a hexagon; but houses have been erected all round the first buildings, and it has now the same appearance as any other town. A railway runs from King William's Town, and there are several good hotels. Queenstown is perhaps the most English town in the colony. The inhabitants have a thorough love and respect for the mother country and its institutions. The railway is being extended to Aliwal and the diamond fields, and there is no doubt, that in a few years Queenstown will become a much more flourishing place than it even now is. We stopped here one day, and then proceeded on our route, passing through a flat country totally devoid of interest, perfectly innocent of all trees, and with water only at intervals from seven to ten miles.

In due time we reached Palmetfontein, a station of the C. M. R. This station is built, like many others in the form of a square, with houses and stables. Nearly the whole troop of C. M. R. were absent, only a few being left to look after the station.

Palmetfontein is distant thirty-five miles from Morosi's

Mountain, and is close to the Orange River. After a day's rest we again marched on, passing between high hills and mountains and fording several small streams, reaching Stork Spruit at night, which consists of a few houses and flour mills. At daylight we reached Silver Spruit, the residence of Mr. Austin, the magistrate. The place is pretty, lying at the foot of a mountain. The house and adjacent buildings were entirely wrecked, as I have mentioned, and the scene looked very desolate. After stopping here for four hours, we again proceeded on our weary way till we reached a place called Thomas's Shop, so named after a store kept by a man of that name. A strong detachment of C. M. R. was stationed here.

At this station was the hospital for the force in the field at Morosi's Mountain. It was fortified with a high stone wall running all round. The buildings were large and commodious, and an experienced medical man and his wife were in charge. Thomas's Shop is about fifteen miles distant from Morosi's Mountain, the road to which place had been entirely made since the commencement of hostilities. It is a tolerably good one, cut out of the side of the hills, but difficult and dangerous to drive in consequence of the sharp turns. In some places there are precipices of 500 feet, over which you would fall sheer into the Orange River should you unluckily get off the road. We did not meet with any mishaps, though we travelled at night, and early at daylight we reached our destination.

The mountain looked blacker than ever, the *schanzes* were increased both in height and number; in fact, the more we looked at it the less we liked it. We found here about 300 C. M. R., with some yeomanry and burghers; our detachment brought the entire force of the C. M. R. up to 350 men, with four guns.

The next day Colonel Bayley arrived to take command, and a few days afterwards the yeomanry, volunteers, burghers, and native levies left for their homes.

This withdrawal of the troops took place on the representation of Colonel Bayley, who declared he would take the mountain with his own regiment, if the Cape government would let him have the direction of affairs and of his own men, unimpeded by others. In this the government wisely acquiesced, and happily he got rid of the irregulars.

We cheered them out of camp as they went away. We felt sorry they were not permitted to participate in the approaching attack, for the men themselves had stuck to their work bravely, and it was not their individual fault that their efforts had been so completely unsuccessful.

After their departure the C. M. R. were formed into one camp on the west side of the mountain, that is, the side facing the slope. A strong stone wall was built round the camp, and immediately below the camp, in a small valley, the horses were kept. We had plenty of food both for ourselves and horses, the commissariat arrangements being now most excellent. The guns were placed in position about a 1000 yards from the first *schanze*, and were daily used whenever a native ventured to show his head. A picket was kept up day and night on the saddle, at a place about 300 yards from the *schanze*, and a lively fusillade used to go on day and night between the besiegers and the besieged, without much damage being done on either side. We let the enemy know we were alive to their designs, and we thus prevented them from descending the mountain to attack the camp.

This picket was changed every twelve hours, and we found it to be most exciting work. The relieving party had to pass within 350 and 400 yards of the firsts *schanze* to reach the Saddle. The enemy were continually on the look-out for us, and peppered away as the men passed, which of course they did at a run. The whole camp used to turn out to watch the relief, and we used to unmercifully chaff our comrades who were about to be shot at. The men got so used to this daily one-sided shooting match, that they took it quite as a matter of course. Our chaff evidently acted as an antidote to the enemy's guns, for not one was on any of these occasions wounded, though the escapes were narrow as well as numerous.

We tried all manner of devices to induce the enemy to attack the camp; but old Morosi was far too cunning to let his men venture into the open. He knew his vantage-ground, and he stuck to it.

We next tried shelling the mountain with the big guns, but without any visible effect. At night-time we used to send up a star shell, which illuminated the whole mountain for half a minute or so. We did this to enable us to get aim with the guns during the duration of the light, and then we fired several rounds in succession. But all this was simply wasting ammunition; and so the colonel appeared to think, for it was soon discontinued.

All we now did was to reconnoitre at night in small parties to find a place suitable for an escalade. It was no secret that this was the plan the colonel and officers had determined to adopt; but the day and time appointed were kept a profound secret. A mortar had been sent for from King William's Town; and scaling-ladders were, we knew, in course of construction at Aliwal.

At last the mortar arrived, with ammunition and equipments. As this mortar helped to a very considerable extent in the taking of the mountain, I will give an account of the difficulties we had to contend with, to make it serviceable and of any use at all. To begin with, it was a service five and a half inch brass mortar, throwing a sixteen pound shell, bursting in the ordinary manner. The mortar was of a very old pattern, and had, I believe, done service at Cape Town, outside the museum with its brother for many years past. It bore the inscription of *George Rex, 1802* on the outside: this will give the reader some idea of the antiquity and value of this remarkable piece of ordnance sent up to us by our old friends, the Cape Town authorities. The fuses which accompanied it had been in store for years, and we thought it advisable to try a few before using them. They were twenty-second fuses. We tried three, and I will detail the interesting results we obtained. Bear in mind they were supposed to burn twenty seconds: the first burnt four seconds, then went off with a shoot; the second would not be persuaded to burn at all and the third burnt five seconds, and then blew out the whole of the composition. We sat down and calmly, or otherwise, and consigned the colonial ordnance to sundry unmentionable places. The result of using these fuses would probably have been the injury or destruction of the entire mortar squad.

We were in a fix. A mortar, plenty of shell and powder, but no fuses. After some consideration and more experiments, we finally, with infinite trouble, transformed a quantity of 7-pounder R. M. L. fuses into mortar fuses, and these we used with perfect success.

A day or so was spent in putting iron bands round the *bed* or carriage of the mortar, and one afternoon we carried this novel piece of ordnance to within 600 yards of the first *schanze*, and commenced a few experimental shots. With these shots we managed to blow a small gap in one of the *schanzes*, when the natives opened such a heavy fire on us, that we were obliged to leave the mortar and take shelter behind some stones, until the guns cleared the *schanzes*, when we retired with the mortar into camp.

I had had some experience with mortars, so this was given into my charge, and I was told to pick a squad of six men to work it, which I soon did. Of course I was careful to select well-trained artillerymen from my own troop.

We had to fire this mortar from a distance of 600 yards from the centre *schanze* of the mountain, and it soon became apparent, that if we did not wish to lose some of our number, a bastion or some protection must be built for the men who were working the mortar. Volunteers were called for, to build. There was no difficulty; forty men at once came forward, and each picking up a big stone at about 800 yards, ran with it to the point determined on for the bastion and deposited it. A sufficient quantity of material being thus collected, we advanced to build. Here the cunning and skill of Morosi significantly displayed itself. Whilst we had been collecting the stones not a shot had been fired by his side, as we were scattered; but directly we were, so to speak, massed, the natives commenced firing at us, volley upon volley. We cheered and piled up the stones, as hard and as quickly as we could, knowing full well the higher we got with the wall the more cover we should enjoy. We were without arms of any description, and within 500 yards of the first *schanze*, when I suppose it suddenly occurred to them for what purpose we were building. Their firing suddenly ceased, and numbers of the enemy appeared on the *schanzes*, as if they intended charging.

But Colonel Bayley had anticipated this, and had pointed the big guns ready for them; with these he soon drove them back. In the interval we had built a bastion twenty feet long, in the form of a semicircle, eight feet high; and to the right of it, about twelve yards distant, the walls of a three-sided house to serve as a powder magazine. We covered this at the top with hides, and over the wall of the bastion a number of hides were hung to prevent the concussion of the mortar knocking the stones down.

At dark that night we brought the mortar up into position, and at daylight astonished the enemy by throwing shell all over the mountain, making several small breaches in the *schanzes*. In fact, to our great joy, and not a little to our surprise, the mortar was a grand success.

For the information of any reader who does not know the difference between the results produced by a projectile fired from a rifled gun, and those of a smooth-bored mortar, a few remarks may not be amiss. The initiated must pardon me making what to them will be a digression. A rifled projectile makes a low trajectory, and consequently loses very little power in traversing the distance it has to go. The shell or shot can only take effect on the side of a *schanze* facing the direction from which the projectile has been fired.

Now, with the mortar the trajectory is high, and the object is to fire the shell so that it will rise a sufficient height and distance only in the air, that by its semi-circular course it may be carried over and inside the *schanzes*. The distinction is illustrated well by a cricket ball, which in one case may be thrown against a wall, while on the other it may be lobbed over it.

Now, our desire was to throw the shells immediately over the *schanzes*, when they would roll down the hill to the men inside, and burst amongst them; and in doing this we made very good practice, which proved most successful.

My mortar squad lived with me in this bastion day and night for five days, and fired at intervals, whenever any of the natives showed themselves. At night we posted a sufficient guard at the bastion in case of attack. But no assault on the bastion was attempted. At night careful surveys had been made of the mountain, and we all knew that we were on the eve of an attack.

The Sunday before the final assault the Bishop of Bloomfontein and two clergymen arrived, and held services in the camp. They were all three Englishmen, and were much appreciated. They went round the camp conversing with the men, and I think we all thought too much praise could not be given to these gentlemen, thus voluntarily leaving their comfortable homes to come and rough it with us for several days as they did, actuated only by the best and kindest of motives—for our encouragement and spiritual welfare. Two days before the attack the Bishop and his chaplain left; but the third clergyman, a Mr. Russell, remained, and went up the mountain with the storming-party to see if he could be of any assistance to the wounded. These kind of men do credit to their country and their cloth, and it is a pity there are not more of the same sort in South Africa.

The scaling-ladders now arrived from Aliwal: they were all too weak, and some too short, while many of them broke with four men on them. They were in thirty feet lengths, well designed, but badly made and put together. We remedied the want of strength by tying two ladders together and strapping them with iron bands.

The day before the attack we amused ourselves with some athletic sports, and in the evening the orders were issued for a general attack the next evening. A reward of £200 was offered for Morosi, alive or dead; the same sum for Dodo; and £25 for the first man on the mountain, with promotion, whether officer or man. It was characteristic of Colonel Bayley that his order began "Morosi's Mountain will be taken tonight by the C. M. R.," &c. Then followed the list of rewards and the disposition of the various troops.

The attack was to take place at the dip of the moon, which was near midnight, about half-past twelve. Parties of six natives were told off to carry the scaling-ladders, of which there were twenty. The men were to dress as they liked, and to arm themselves in any way they fancied; but all, without exception, were to carry their carbines and revolvers. These orders, with a few more details respecting the time the mortar and big guns were to begin and cease firing, constituted the instructions under which we were to proceed to attack this redoubtable stronghold.

For four days and nights previous to the attack the mortar had been constantly fired, at intervals of ten minutes at night time and varied intervals in the day, generally leaving off for about four hours to enable the mortar squad to obtain a little rest. The mortar was worked by the same squad all through this time, and we were beginning to be thoroughly knocked up. The guns were to fire at intervals during the day preceding the attack, and both guns and mortar were to cease firing at twelve at night. The attempt to get on the mountain was to be made by scaling-ladders up the fissure called Bourne's Crack, which I have described, and the *krantz* immediately surrounding it. Then officers were told off to lead the storming-parties at these several points. During the day previous to the attack twenty-five men of a force called the Woodhouse Border Guard, under Lieutenant Mulenbeck, and fifty Fingoes under Captain Hook, the magistrate at Herschel, and Allan Maclean, arrived. The whole force to attack the mountain numbered between 350 and 400 white men, and about 100 natives.

As the day wore on the guns and mortar continued to fire at intervals, as ordered, and our men were lying about on the ground in all directions.

The camp presented a strange spectacle: some laughing and talking, others playing cards, others writing letters; but underlying all this apparent indifference to the future, an acute observer could note that much of the merriment was forced, and that nearly all were anxious as to the result of the game to be played that night.

The force which was prepared to attack this evening was less than half in number to that which had previously tried and twice been beaten back, with heavy loss each time. No wonder there were many anxious faces, thinking probably more than they had ever yet thought in their lives.

At sunset the picket on the Saddle were relieved by Lieutenant Mulenbeck and his men. Their orders were to hold the Saddle, and try to get into the *schanzes* as soon as the attack began—a bold and perilous undertaking. At 11 p.m. all the tents in camp were struck, and the men fell in noiselessly and in silence; and with a hearty "good luck" from the artillerymen at the guns, they started on their way to the foot of the mountain, some 1500 yards distant.

Whilst this storming-party was marching to the point of attack, a strong breastwork was built in one corner of the camp, constructed with casks and bags of *mealies*. This was a precaution in case of a repulse, to afford a place of shelter to which the men might retreat. An additional reason for this arose out of a report by some Fingoes, that a party of about 200 Tambookies, who had come in during the evening, were going to attack the camp directly the storming detachment left it.

Though these Tambookies were nominally friendly to the Cape government, and had professedly come in to assist; yet, as their home is on the borders of Basutoland, it was highly probable that, in the event of the storming-party meeting with a repulse, they would act as reported. Had they so done, they would have met with a very agreeable reception.

The signal to the storming-party to proceed was to be the firing of three rockets in quick succession. The storming-parties were then to go forward as arranged; and these Tambookies were ordered to ascend a gully to the left of the slope and facing the camp, when the guns and mortars had ceased firing, and the mortar detachment was to join the storming-party. From this part of the arrangement there was obliged to be a deviation, for the bed of the mortar had been getting shaky all day, and at 10.30 that night finally collapsed, rendering the mortar useless. It had done, however, good service, and had fired 367 rounds of shell on the mountain during the four days and nights it had been kept at work.

The rockets went up, and the storming-party placed their ladders and commenced climbing up. Lieutenant Springer of No. 3 troop planted his ladder to the right of Bourne's Crack, and with his men climbed up. When near the top a native put his head over the *krantz* and said to him in Dutch, "Don't come up here, or I'll shoot you."

"Shoot away," said Springer; and the native, looking over, exposed too much of his body, and was shot by Springer himself, the bullet from the native grazing the lieutenant's shoulder and going through his shirt.

These shots aroused the whole mountain; but our men were now fast getting up the ladders, and as it happened, the enemy were all in the *schanzes*, expecting we should attack the same way as hitherto. There were only about thirty of the enemy on this side, and they were speedily shot down. Five minutes after the ladders had been planted 200 men were on the mountain, and helping the remainder up. Mulenbeck, in the mean time, from the Saddle had fought his way up with his men, and had reached the fourth *schanze*, after shooting down the enemy in the previous *schanzes*, through which and over which we had come.

The Fingoes had also reached the top of the gully, headed by Allan Maclean. The Tambookies had refused to go on, and Captain Hook had marched them back, and they were disarmed by the artillery and made prisoners.

Let me now return to the storming-party. A few minutes after the first 200 men were up, the remainder had all been pulled up somehow or other. Nearly all the ladders had broken, owing to the excitement of the men who had crowded on them.

Nearly all the enemy had by this time come over from the *schanzes* and the opposite side of the mountain to resist the storming-party. Forming in line, and cheering heartily, the C. M. R. charged across the flat top of the mountain, driving the enemy in front of them. For a few brief minutes it was hand to hand, and then the natives were cut down and shot where they stood, those that escaped only to be driven over the perpendicular sides of the mountain and smashed to pieces in their fall. The C. M. R. were now divided into three parties, and commenced scouring out all the nooks and crannies for Morosi and Dodo.

Small parties of Baphutis were found hidden in various caves, and were immediately brought out and shot; and at last, after several attempts to get inside a cave where Morosi was found to be, he was shot, but Dodo could nowhere be discovered.

At five o'clock a.m., just as the sun was rising, the Union Jack was hoisted on the top of the highest point of the mountain, and in half-an-hour afterwards Morosi's head was placed on a staff in the centre of our camp, a ghastly warning to all rebels.

Morosi, the old chief, was shot by a private in the C. M. R.

named Whitehead, who had a narrow escape, the bullet Morosi fired at him going straight through the peak and crown of his cap. Whitehead did not know he had shot Morosi, and when the body was brought down by one of the Woodhouse Border Guard, he of course received the reward, which was rather hard on Whitehead.

Our loss in this action was two men severely wounded, one Fingoe killed by an accidental shot from one of his own party, and one wounded. The enemy lost heavily; four old women, Morosi's wives, two children, and one paralyzed man constituted the prisoners taken, all the rest were either killed or had escaped.

The prisoners assured us there were 500 men on the day before the attack, but that at this time there were not more than 300. Morosi and his sons, except Dodo, were killed, and about 200 of his men. Dodo and about 120 men escaped by throwing themselves into the Orange River. How many were killed in that desperate leap it is impossible to say.

The Tambookies who had refused to join in the attack were stripped, flogged, and driven out of camp. This was the last we saw of them.

Such was the capture of Morosi's Mountain, taken by a surprise, well conceived and as well executed, reflecting great credit on Colonel Bayley, who did not, however, stop to thank us, but hurried off the field to the colony to receive the acknowledgments of the government and colony at large.

Morosi in this mountain had for nine months successfully defied all efforts to compel him to evacuate his position, costing the government many good lives and a great deal of money. No wonder the government made much of Colonel Bayley. He was our colonel, and we had to be satisfied with this, for it was all the thanks the force ever received. Civil words cost nothing, and the government might have taken the trouble to thank the men of the C. M. R. for the victory. It was by their pluck, and by them alone, that Morosi's Mountain was taken; for, as a matter of fact, Colonel Bayley and the adjutant were never on the mountain at all, either in the attack or subsequently.

CHAPTER 19

Promotions

The scene on the top of Morosi's Mountain after it was taken is almost impossible to describe. In every direction dead men, women, and children lying where they had been shot. Nearly all the women and children had been killed by pieces of the mortar shells. The prisoners told us that the mortar and guns drove them mad; go where they would, they could not get out of the way of these bits of iron flying about in every direction.

On the top of the mountain was a square house, strongly built of stone, and containing six or seven tons of gunpowder. Cattle, dead and dying, were lying about, together with immense quantities of bones. There were many springs of good water, and abundance of corn; and with the quantity of food collected there, the enemy could, without doubt, have held out for a long time.

After a day's rest we all set to work to demolish the *schanzes*, and clear up the mountain for occupation. A troop of C. M. R. was kept continually on the top, and relieved every twenty-four hours. The powder magazine was blown up, and the dead cleared off the top. In a week's time the flat presented quite a decent and respectable appearance.

Fourteen days after the date of the capture the whole of the artillery were ordered to go to Ibeka. Two troops of C. M. R. accompanied us as far as Queenstown, and at that point we separated for our different stations.

At Queenstown we were entertained with a public dinner and an address from the mayor and corporation, and the force was treated with the greatest kindness and hospitality.

In due time we reached Ibeka, having been twenty-two days on the road; but shortly after our arrival it was determined to shift the head-quarters of the C. M. R. to King William's Town, and also to transfer the whole of the Artillery in time to that town. Meanwhile half the troop marched down to King William's Town, and I remained at Ibeka with about twenty men of the artillery corps.

The period for which I had taken service was now drawing to a close. Much discontent prevailed in the force, consequent on the promotions which were daily being made. The selections reflected, with few exceptions, no credit on Colonel Bayley, and cost the force many valuable men, who retired because they were overlooked; these men had served for a long time, and through the whole of the war, and were on all hands acknowledged to have done good service for years past. These men eventually left in disgust at their treatment. Men who had never been out of the head-quarters office, or had seen a shot fired, who had a comfortable time of it from the date of joining, were made non-commissioned officers. This was our old grievance in the F. A. M. Police days, that the office men were so frequently promoted. Unjust as this was felt to be by the men who had been actively engaged in the force, it would not have mattered so much if they had been kept to scribble away as before; but they were distributed in their new rank amongst the troops, totally ignorant of the duties which devolved on them, unable to keep a duty-roll, or drill a squad of men, and they were of course held up to ridicule by the force in general for their incompetency.

It would have been supposed that a military man like our colonel would have avoided the error committed too frequently in the old police days; but he steadily kept in the former impolitic groove.

With regard to the officers, he made promotions which were far worse. First of all, an examination was started for the rank of lieutenant. I will guarantee that even a school-boy could pass it in England.

Seven selections from the rank and file were made for this examination. Let me refer in detail to their services and social qualities. The reader will, I think, be edified by some of these instances.

No. 1 was a gentleman by birth and education. He had served six years in the force, and for thirteen months had served as sergeant. He passed, and was subsequently killed in the Basuto war. The only objection to him was, that he was far too young and inexperienced to command men; but he was the best in list of selections, and otherwise unexceptionable.

No. 2 was made of very raw material, and was entirely without education. He could not pretend to the simplest rudiments even of an education. He was universally disliked by the force. He had a loud voice and a bullying, blustering manner. He was selected by the adjutant to be drill-instructor. He had been a sergeant about ten months. He did not pass.

No. 3 was a gentleman, but had only been two and a half years in the force. He had never served as sergeant or out of the ranks, and was notoriously the most troublesome man in his troop. Nevertheless, he was fairly educated, and a great improvement on No. 2.

No. 4 had been a sergeant for three years, but was very imperfectly educated. He had plenty of bounce, was a smart non-com.; but in no way fitted to be a commissioned officer. He did not pass, but was promoted to sergeant-major, for which position he was admirably fitted in every way.

No. 5 was totally uneducated. At home he had been an engine-driver. He had been a sergeant for two years. He did not pass.

No. 6 had a good education, but failed to pass in drill and evolutions.

No. 7 was a boy of eighteen, who had been promoted to sergeant the day before in order that he might go up for this examination. His mother was a very fine woman, and his sisters were considered pretty. He had been in the office nearly all the time he had served, and was about as much fitted to be a parson as an officer.

Such were the selections made by the officer in command. No wonder that great discontent prevailed in the force. No doubt promotion by merit is full of difficulty; but there were plenty of men in the force who had served in cavalry regiments at home, both as officers and non-coms.—men who thoroughly understood their drill and duties, who were well educated, and in every way fit for the position of officers. Why these men were passed over to make way for so doubtful a lot no one could understand; they knew nothing and could do nothing; they have been the laughing-stock with all the men left in the ranks ever since their promotions. The reason seems to be, that if properly qualified men had been selected, they would have gradually supplanted the useless police officers who remained; and this did not suit the views of the colonel or adjutant, the latter being quite as unfit for his position as the majority of the police officers, and in some respects inferior even to these.

But these promotions I have mentioned were as nothing compared with more which were to follow. A batch of men were made into officers, for no apparent reason. One of these was a private in the artillery troop. He was the most troublesome and useless creature it is possible to conceive. He was always late for parade, perpetually in the defaulter list, never clean, and always disreputable-looking. Judge of my surprise when, after I had left the force, I saw his name one day in the *Gazette* as lieutenant. This man, unless totally changed, could have been promoted for no other reason than that he made 108 runs at cricket in a match between the eleven of King William's Town and Port Elizabeth. Did he contrive to get into the colonel's good books, and was given a commission, as an encouragement to his late comrades to be as dirty and slovenly as himself?

Another promotion was that of a man who could sing well at the concerts which were frequently given by the C. M. R. I was personally acquainted with this man, and know that he never did a day's service the whole time, from the day of his entry into the force to the time of his promotion. Whenever he was ordered anywhere he always fell sick, or alleged he was sick; in fact, he was nothing more nor less than a regular schemer. For the last year he had been employed in the head-quarters office, where he had learned to play a decent game of quoits, and this amusement he used frequently to enjoy with the colonel, who was fond of quoits, and hence perhaps his promotion.

Another promotion was more extraordinary still. In the early part of my narrative I mentioned that one of our party absconded at Port Elizabeth. After being absent four months, and being unable to obtain employment, he came to King William's Town, full of penitence, and gave himself up as a deserter. A war was then being carried on with the Galekas; he was merely fined and sent up to No. 9 troop, with which he served through the war. At the termination of these hostilities he was transferred to the Artillery Troop, where he succeeded in obtaining for himself a snug little berth in the post-office, stopping in it for many months. When the artillery was ordered up to Morosi's Mountain he went up with us, and remained until shortly after the second attack, when he returned with the rest of his troop to Ibeka, and took no part in the capture. His father, it appears, holds a high position in the Royal Artillery, and with this interest he obtained a commission, over the heads of men who have been six years or more in the Artillery Troop, and who were qualified in every way. Was his promotion due to his having been always a troublesome character, that he had this particular interest I have mentioned, which countervailed the fact of his being a deserter, or what were the merits which qualified him for a commission?

I need not trouble the reader with any more instances of the injustice and unfairness of these promotions, which, I regret to testify, were of frequent occurrence. I have dwelt on them only to call attention to the impolicy of such a course. I could fill pages, would it not prove irksome, with instances of this glaring impolicy and wrong. But I trust I have stated enough to justify what I have said with regard to the persistent mismanagement of a highly deserving and meritorious force.

As far as I was personally concerned, these promotions did not affect me very much. I had always intended to leave at the expiration of my period of three years' service; but it would have been a gracious act, which I should have valued, to have offered me something after the service it was acknowledged I had rendered. I had been several times mentioned in despatches for special service, and particularly for service successfully carried through at the storming of Morosi's Mountain. I am content with the knowledge that I had done my duty. I applied for a month's leave and my discharge, and was offered further promotion if I would remain and re-engage; but I had seen too much of such promises, and could not trust them.

I wished to settle down somewhere near Umtata, where I had made some friends. I therefore told the colonel I determined to leave, and I eventually obtained my discharge.

I have now brought this narrative of three years' service in the C. M. R. to a close. I left the service, very sorry to part with my old comrades, with whom I had spent many happy days, and by whose side I had been through many thrilling and fearful scenes.

May they all prosper in their various positions, and spend as happy a time in South Africa as did the writer!

CHAPTER 20

Conclusion

I had now left the force, taking many pleasing recollections of the past with me, and not a few remembrances of many hardships and perils through which I had passed. I had travelled on various duties all over the country, and had made many friends. I pitched upon Umtata as a resting-place, it being already a rising town, and there was not as yet the same amount of severe competition which prevailed in other parts of the colony.

I had gained a tolerable knowledge of the Kaffir language, and had formed various ideas of trading with the natives, principally gathered whilst I had been stationed at St. Johns River. In addition to these recommendations, Umtata is thoroughly English. Many members of my old corps had settled in these parts, which was a further inducement; to live amongst them was not like going amongst perfect strangers.

I had a little capital, and I bought a wagon and a span of oxen, engaged a couple of Kaffirs to help me to work them, and proceeded to Umtata. I went into partnership with a man who had been in No. 6 troop F. A. M. Police, who had been settled some eighteen months or so at a place about ten miles from Umtata. He too had a wagon and some oxen, and a nice farm, and we worked here and prospered for some months.

We erected a good home, with stables and outbuildings, fenced in a good bit of land, and put it under cultivation. All our work was for nothing, however, for we were in a short time burnt out by the Kaffirs, losing everything we possessed, the writer narrowly escaping with his life.

How this happened I may briefly relate.

To the north-east of our farm lay the countries of Umhonholo and Umditswa, chiefs of the Pondomise. The magistrate with the former was Mr. Hope, and with the latter Mr. Welsh. When the war with the Basutos broke out, owing to the attempt of the Cape government to disarm their tribe, Mr. Hope, the resident magistrate with Umhonholo, was requested by the government to raise a native contingent of Umhonholo's Pondomise to assist the government to carry on the war against the Basutos. In the beginning of October, about 900 guns, with abundance of ammunition, were sent to Mr. Hope's residency that he might arm these Pondomise. Two of Major Elliot's clerks were to accompany Mr. Hope as officers, and they proceeded to Ghimbu, where Mr. Hope's house stood.

The day before the arming of this contingent, Umhonholo invited Mr. Hope and Messrs. Warren and Henman, the two clerks to whom I refer, to witness a war-dance of his tribe. Mr. Hope seems to have anticipated that some mischief was intended, as he told Warren and Henman not to come with him unless they liked.

"I must myself attend," he said; "it is too late now to go back, and besides, the orders from Cape Town are urgent that I should raise this contingent."

Warren and Henman refused to let him go by himself; so they went with Mr. Hope to Umhonholo's "Great Place" to see this dance. Mr. Davis, Mr. Hope's clerk, also accompanied the party. What took place I will quote as near as possible in Mr. Davis's words. He was the only one of the whole party that escaped. Mr. Hope and his party arrived on the ground where the army of Umhonholo was. Umhonholo at once invited them to sit down, which they did. The dance then began, the Kaffirs gradually forming a circle round them and as gradually closing in on them. When they were within twelve yards or so of Mr. Hope and his party, Umhonholo rose and came to me, saying, "I want to speak to you outside the circle."

He took my arm, and I went with him; when about twenty yards from the outside a fearful yell arose, and looking round, I saw Messrs. Hope and Warren and Henman held aloft on the points of *assegais*. A number of the Kaffirs then came round me; but Umhonholo, throwing his arms round me, said I should not be killed, as I was the brother of a missionary, and also the son of one who had always been a friend to him. Thus this treacherous murder was accomplished. Mr. Davis escaped in safety to Umtata, and the whole country was in a blaze.

It appears that Mr. Davis asked Umhonholo why he had permitted this murder, and his reply was he wanted to kill government, that government was getting too strong for him; but there is no doubt the sight of the guns and ammunition which had been sent to Mr. Hope was too strong for him. Directly the murder had been perpetrated he possessed himself of them all. One extraordinary incident in this tragedy was, that one of the wagons and span of oxen which had brought the arms belonged to a trader in Pondoland. Umhonholo sent these back intact to the owner, with a message that he was not fighting the white man, but only the government. However, after this outrage the white man very soon began to fight him.

The tragedy I have related happened on Oct. 23, 1880, on a Sunday, and the next day all the trading stores and stations in Pondomiseland were in flames, and the owners flying for their lives to Umtata. My partner, with his wife, sister, and the writer were at breakfast, when a man came galloping in on a horse white with foam, telling us what had occurred, and urging us immediately to go into Umtata, as the Kaffirs were overrunning the country. The whole party accordingly went in except myself, leaving everything just as it stood. My friend had not been gone twenty minutes before the Kaffirs descended in force, and made me a prisoner, tying me up. They proceeded to pillage the house and buildings, and having completely gutted them, they burnt the whole dwelling to the ground. Fortunately for me there was in the store a good deal of "Cape smoke" on which they all got very drunk, and thus overlooked me. At dark some of my Kaffir boys found me and released me. They provided me with a horse, on which I went to Umtata, having myself travelled these ten intervening miles in, I flatter myself, the quickest time on record.

A shirt and a pair of old trousers was what remained to me as my sole possessions. I was, in fact, ruined, as likewise my friend and partner was. In Umtata a *laager* was being formed, and all the women and children taken into it. A scene of the direst confusion prevailed, impossible to realize or describe.

Major Elliot, the chief magistrate, had called a public meeting, and measures were being taken under his admirable guidance to render the place secure. Volunteer corps were formed, and all the available arms and ammunition were distributed. They fell sadly short of our need. The magazine had been almost entirely denuded of arms, and the ammunition was nearly all gone; and when every available rifle was brought to light we could muster no more than twenty guns for the use of about 250 men.

All day long people were *trekking* in with their wives and families, and when evening closed large bodies of Kaffirs appeared on the hills over the Umtata, apparently waiting to attack us. With the *laager* only half built we passed an anxious night, and when morning dawned the Kaffirs were still in view, their number largely augmented.

On the Pondoland side of Umtata stand a few houses distant about a mile from each other, and on these houses the Kaffirs descended, pillaging and destroying everything. The owners with their families had passed the previous night in these houses, thinking that as they were in Pondoland they would be safe, a too fallacious opinion, as it proved. At daylight they came over the river into the *laager*, and we had the mortification of watching these natives plunder and burn everything without being able to lift a hand to prevent them. About three o'clock flesh and blood would stand the sight no longer, and a party of twenty of us crossed the river and charged the Kaffirs, who fled, dropping everything they had stolen. We shot four of them and captured three horses, but the destruction of the houses was complete.

For nearly half a mile the ground was strewn with plunder. Everything was spoilt, and very little was recovered by the owners. Now as these houses were in Pondoland and under the protection of Umquiliso, we began to think that the Pondos intended to join this outbreak. Major Elliot now formed three corps of mounted men—one corps to act as an intelligence corps, and the other two as garrison corps.

The first-mentioned had instructions to go about at night and in the day-time when they could, and ascertain the whereabouts of the enemy. In this corps all were young men who had lost heavily in these disastrous occurrences. They were all well mounted and equipped, and could all ride and shoot to perfection. In the discharge of their duties they went through some very narrow escapes, and had generally an exciting time of it. This corps was commanded by an artillery sergeant of the C. M. R. who had lately taken his discharge.

The other two corps were composed of the remainder of the inhabitants of Umtata, with a few Hottentots intermixed, and did excellent service both in garrison and in short expeditions against the enemy afterwards. One corps was commanded by an old sergeant of police, and the other by a clerk of Major Elliot's; the former knew their work, and of course the latter could not be expected to know much, and did not. It was a pity that some man more suitable was not available for the second corps, as it afterwards hampered the movements of the other two corps through the inefficiency of this commander. A week after the outbreak the *laager* was completed. We boarded up outside the wagons about eight feet and made loopholes. The Kaffirs, though still threatening, did not attack Umtata for some reason we never knew. At last an ample supply of guns and ammunition arrived, together with a party of C. M. R. and volunteer artillery. From this time Umtata was considered safe, and, in fact, was safe, for it was never attacked.

Gangeliswe came in and told us he was utterly unable to control his tribe, that he was afraid they would break out. This they soon afterwards did, pillaging and ransacking the stores in every direction. In the meantime Mr. Welsh, the magistrate of Umditswa, resident at Tsolo, had taken refuge in his gaol, and had fortified himself within its walls, with a small supply of food and about 300 rounds of ammunition. To relieve him at any cost was felt to be necessary, and negotiations were set on foot with Umquiliso to ascertain if he would assist; but it was very uncertain whether he could be trusted, because he had already allowed the traders to be pillaged and their places to be burnt whilst being under his protection. It was also thought that it was simply a ruse to obtain more guns and ammunition, and that after the relieving party had proceeded some way they would be killed. In this difficult position, where it was impossible to spare any large body of men from Umtata, Major Elliot decided to entrust the duty of relief to volunteers.

Volunteers were accordingly called for, from whom six men were selected, all belonging to the intelligence corps, except one man, who was the captain of one of the garrison corps. Mr. Morris, a missionary, also volunteered to accompany the expedition, and his services were accepted. His intimate knowledge of the language and the people would be found of great use.

No doubt this expedition was one of a most dangerous character. It was felt in Umtata that the chances were greatly against any of the party ever coming back. The expedition, however, succeeded after many and great difficulties, and released Mr. Welsh and thirty-four men, women, and children, bringing them safely into Umtata. Great was the joy when they arrived. How they had accomplished their dangerous and difficult task is described in the official report I append.

The Relief of Mr. Welsh

Subjoined are the Particulars, *In Extenso* as Contained in the Report of this Event

To Major Elliot
C. At. C, Chief Magistrate, &c, &c.
Umtata, Nov. 1, 1880
Sir,
I have the honour to report that, acting under your instructions, I proceeded on Saturday morning last for the relief of Mr. Welsh, the magistrate of Tsolo, with the following men under my command, *viz*.: John Vice, Joseph Vice, R. Cowie, A. Lowder, and T. Mathews. The Rev. Mr.

Morris also accompanied the expedition, and undertook all negotiations and arrangements with the various chiefs and headsmen through whose country we had to pass.

Upon arrival at the Gongubulu we found only the men belonging to Mr. Morris's mission-station, instead of some 300 men which we expected, and which had been promised by the chief N'Quiliso.

After consultation with Mr. Morris and Philip Charles, one of N'Quiliso's councillors, we proceeded to a *kraal* three miles further on, and there found Xambella, N'Quiliso's brother, who told us, after some conversation, that we had better wait the arrival of the army, which might arrive or might not. Mr. Morris informed him that we had not come there to wait, but to proceed with him and his army, and that if he did not call out his men we should return to Umtata. After very great delay and threatening on our part to return, Xambella at last reluctantly consented to call out his men, on condition that we should wait until the following morning; and this I consented to do.

Shortly afterwards, I found in a hut one of Umditswa's chief councillors. This man I made prisoner, and detained as a hostage. During the night the chief, N'Quiliso, arrived, and about 150 men, with a few of the principal Pondoland traders. I *spanned* in at 8 a. m., and proceeded for Tsolo with about 150 to 200 Pondos.

After getting round St Paul's (Cheknoxa) several scouts were seen on the surrounding hills, and as we proceeded, the "war-cry" was sounded, and about an hour afterwards small bodies of men were seen galloping towards Umditswa's "Great Place," at this time about three miles distant. On approaching the "Great Place" two natives were despatched by request of Philip Charles to inform Umditswa that we were going to relieve Mr. Welsh, and request that we should not be disturbed or interrupted. These men returned shortly afterwards, bringing with them two of Umditswa's sons and a few of his principal councillors, for the purpose, as they said, of showing us the way.

I arrived at Tsolo at 1.45 p. m., and outspanned. I was at the same time informed by a Pondo that their men were going to stop us removing fourteen guns and ammunition, and that an attack would be made upon us if we tried to remove them. Upon receipt of this intelligence, and after verifying the same, I immediately made prisoners of the whole party, and placed fifteen Pondos, principally petty chiefs of N'Quiliso, to guard them, with strict instructions to prevent them crossing the Tsolo, and if they in any way attempted to alarm the country to shoot them down. These Pondos were well armed with snider carbines, and were perfectly able to carry the order into effect.

We then proceeded across the river with about 100 Pondos and all the traders to the gaol of the Tsolo Magistracy, distant about three-quarters of a mile. Considerable delay occurred through Mr. Welsh and his clerk, Mr. Cummings, refusing to leave, and I had to very thoroughly explain my orders to Mr. Welsh before he at last evacuated the prison with the following persons, thirty-five souls in all, *viz.*:— Mr. Welsh, Mrs. Welsh, Miss Welsh, seven children, Mr. Cummings, the Rev. Cameron, the Rev. Stuart, Mrs. Stuart, one child and European female servant, Mr. Leary, Mrs. Leary and five children, James Maskell, Hall Douglass, W. Shepstone, A. G. Brown, J. Hudson, Peter Ellse, one native interpreter, four policemen (natives), one native servant.

I escorted Mr. Welsh to the wagon myself, and the oxen having been previously *spanned* in, proceeded immediately for Umtata.

From spies and others that I had information from, I found that the enemy, principally Umhonholo's people, were collecting at the Tsolo Bush (N'Qwenki), immediately at the back of the Residency; and I was consequently very anxious, with my small force, to reach St Paul's before dark, where the open country would have given us a better advantage. I stationed the reserve men in various parts of the column, and made every possible arrangement for successfully resisting an attack.

The enemy still continued to collect in every direction, but were kept back by messages from the hostages not to approach us, or they would be shot. At St. Paul's a terrible thunderstorm delayed us for an hour. During the journey back, small bodies of Pondos joined the column, but the whole number never exceeded 700 or 800 men, going out never more than 200.

Great difficulty on the way back was experienced in preventing the Pondos from plundering, and I beg here to call your attention to the great assistance given me by the Pondo traders, who, one and all, helped me in carrying your orders on that head into effect.

We reached the *kraal* we had slept at the previous night at 1.30 in the morning, and the hostages were here released; we *spanned* in again at eight, and reached Umtata at twelve.

The expedition was away from Umtata exactly fifty hours, and during that time travelled fifty-eight miles.

The horses were twenty-two consecutive hours under the saddle, and the oxen twenty-one hours in the yoke, only being *out-spanned* one hour at Tsolo. I wish to call your attention to the excellent arrangements made by Mr. Morris for commissariat and transport; every comfort and necessary was provided by his diligence and forethought. I feel certain that without his very valuable assistance, his cool courage, and the splendid way that he kept the Pondos and chiefs in order, the expedition would not have so successfully been brought to a conclusion.

Of the five men I had the great honour to command, they behaved as you expected them to do, and they share with me the deep feeling of thankfulness that we have been able to rescue a lot of helpless men, women, and children from the hands of merciless and barbarous savages.—I have, &c,

Alex. Granville

In command of Tsolo Relief Expedition

Mr. Welsh and his party were in the most destitute condition, having only the clothes they stood in. They had lost everything they had in the world. One man, the owner of five stations, had all burnt to the ground, besides losing a valuable stock of cattle and sheep. The church and mission-station at St. Augustine's was burnt to the ground, and most of the mission Kaffirs killed.

A large force of white men was now raised in the Cape colony, and also in Natal. These forces were concentrated towards Umtata, and quickly cleared the country of rebels. Immense quantities of cattle were captured, and numbers of rebels killed. The fighting was in some cases desperate, and no quarter was given or expected. Umditswa at last being hemmed in on every side gave himself up, but Umhonholo evaded capture, and eventually escaped through the mountains and joined the Pondos.

I may as well here finish with Umquiliso, the chief of the Pondos. His tribe never openly broke out, but there can be no doubt they rendered great assistance to the Pondomise, receiving and taking care of their women and the cattle.

Umquiliso himself does not want to fight, and it is with the greatest difficulty that he restrains his people from hostilities. Fight they will, sooner or later. I regard it as a mere question of a few years before war will again happen, the result of which must be that the whole of Pondoland will be annexed to the colony. I am pretty sure that the best and wisest policy would be for the government to settle this question at once, and not leave it to be answered hereafter when a few years may have elapsed.

In February, 1881, there were close upon 15,000 white men in the field, and this rebellion of the Pondomise was crushed, through the promptitude of the Cape government in pouring in a sufficient quantity of white forces to check the outbreak at its commencement.

The farmers and traders were beginning to return to the remains of their farm-houses, and the country round about Umtata was beginning to assume a more settled aspect.

The difficulties with which the chief Magistrate of Umtata, Major Elliot, had to contend at the beginning of this rebellion can only be known and appreciated by those who were in Umtata at the time of the outbreak. Without a sufficient quantity of men, arms, or ammunition, and totally cut off from supplies, he established and organized a force that struck terror into the Kaffirs from the commencement of the rebellion, and saved the Cape colony from another war, which the general outbreak of the whole of the native tribes would have produced. That his efforts, and the results which have accrued from them, will meet with due reward from the government is the hope of every one in Umtata.

I had now no home to go to, and the country being quiet, and letters from England arrived urging me to return, I accordingly left for the old country; and after a prosperous voyage of twenty-eight days from Port Elizabeth, arrived at Plymouth in March, having been absent four years within a few days. I returned home not without opinions I had formed of the Kaffirs, and the way to manage them. They are strongly impressed in my mind, but would hardly interest the reader. They do not differ very much in respect of the mode of improving the natives from that of the American with regard to the Indians, whom he would have improved off the face of the earth.

What to do, or how to govern the hordes of savages who overrun the Cape colony, is a problem that will take a far wiser head than mine to solve; but one thing is certain, that in whatever way the future government of the colony decide to deal with the natives, success of any kind can only be insured by contriving some well-devised policy with a steady and unvarying hand. The vacillation and uncertainty of the past must cease. A firm and liberal policy, persistently going on in the same direction and with the same aims, will tend far better to soften and subdue the Kaffir and bring him under the domination of the white men, than any of the alternately fast and loose methods which have prevailed in years past. The assertion of superiority is utterly indispensable, or we had better come away.

In conclusion, I have endeavoured to lay before the reader what life in the C. M. R. is. I served through troublesome times when the corps was in a period of transition; very undisciplined when I joined as a private, greatly improved when I retired, as a second-class sergeant. I would recommend any young fellow who thought of settling in South Africa to begin by joining this service. During the period of his military life he would see many places and parts of the colony hardly otherwise accessible. He would make many friends, and gain in the easiest way considerable knowledge of the country in which he contemplated making his home. The C. M. R. is now a popular force in the colony, is tolerably well officered, well treated and looked after in every way, different in these respects compared with its earlier condition. If I have succeeded in interesting the reader by narrating what I went through during the few years of service I passed in South Africa, I shall not be altogether unrewarded.

LEONAUR

ALSO FROM LEONAUR

AVAILABLE IN SOFTCOVER OR HARDCOVER WITH DUST JACKET

JOURNALS OF ROBERT ROGERS OF THE RANGERS *by Robert Rogers*—The exploits of Rogers & the Rangers in his own words during 1755-1761 in the French & Indian War.

GALLOPING GUNS *by James Young*—The Experiences of an Officer of the Bengal Horse Artillery During the Second Maratha War 1804-1805.

GORDON *by Demetrius Charles Boulger*—The Career of Gordon of Khartoum.

THE BATTLE OF NEW ORLEANS *by Zachary F. Smith*—The final major engagement of the War of 1812.

THE TWO WARS OF MRS DUBERLY *by Frances Isabella Duberly*—An Intrepid Victorian Lady's Experience of the Crimea and Indian Mutiny.

WITH THE GUARDS' BRIGADE DURING THE BOER WAR *by Edward P. Lowry*—On Campaign from Bloemfontein to Koomati Poort and Back.

THE REBELLIOUS DUCHESS *by Paul F. S. Dermoncourt*—The Adventures of the Duchess of Berri and Her Attempt to Overthrow French Monarchy.

MEN OF THE MUTINY *by John Tulloch Nash & Henry Metcalfe*—Two Accounts of the Great Indian Mutiny of 1857: Fighting with the Bengal Yeomanry Cavalry & Private Metcalfe at Lucknow.

CAMPAIGN IN THE CRIMEA *by George Shuldham Peard*—The Recollections of an Officer of the 20th Regiment of Foot.

WITHIN SEBASTOPOL *by K. Hodasevich*—A Narrative of the Campaign in the Crimea, and of the Events of the Siege.

WITH THE CAVALRY TO AFGHANISTAN *by William Taylor*—The Experiences of a Trooper of H. M. 4th Light Dragoons During the First Afghan War.

THE CAWNPORE MAN *by Mowbray Thompson*—A First Hand Account of the Siege and Massacre During the Indian Mutiny By One of Four Survivors.

BRIGADE COMMANDER: AFGHANISTAN *by Henry Brooke*—The Journal of the Commander of the 2nd Infantry Brigade, Kandahar Field Force During the Second Afghan War.

BANCROFT OF THE BENGAL HORSE ARTILLERY *by N. W. Bancroft*—An Account of the First Sikh War 1845-1846.

LEONAUR

ALSO FROM LEONAUR
AVAILABLE IN SOFTCOVER OR HARDCOVER WITH DUST JACKET

THE 2ND MAORI WAR: 1860-1861 *by Robert Carey*—The Second Maori War, or First Taranaki War, one more bloody instalment of the conflicts between European settlers and the indigenous Maori people.

A JOURNAL OF THE SECOND SIKH WAR *by Daniel A. Sandford*—The Experiences of an Ensign of the 2nd Bengal European Regiment During the Campaign in the Punjab, India, 1848-49.

THE LIGHT INFANTRY OFFICER *by John H. Cooke*—The Experiences of an Officer of the 43rd Light Infantry in America During the War of 1812.

BUSHVELDT CARBINEERS *by George Witton*—The War Against the Boers in South Africa and the 'Breaker' Morant Incident.

LAKE'S CAMPAIGNS IN INDIA *by Hugh Pearse*—The Second Anglo Maratha War, 1803-1807.

BRITAIN IN AFGHANISTAN 1: THE FIRST AFGHAN WAR 1839-42 *by Archibald Forbes*—From invasion to destruction-a British military disaster.

BRITAIN IN AFGHANISTAN 2: THE SECOND AFGHAN WAR 1878-80 *by Archibald Forbes*—This is the history of the Second Afghan War-another episode of British military history typified by savagery, massacre, siege and battles.

UP AMONG THE PANDIES *by Vivian Dering Majendie*—Experiences of a British Officer on Campaign During the Indian Mutiny, 1857-1858.

MUTINY: 1857 *by James Humphries*—Authentic Voices from the Indian Mutiny-First Hand Accounts of Battles, Sieges and Personal Hardships.

BLOW THE BUGLE, DRAW THE SWORD *by W. H. G. Kingston*—The Wars, Campaigns, Regiments and Soldiers of the British & Indian Armies During the Victorian Era, 1839-1898.

WAR BEYOND THE DRAGON PAGODA *by Major J. J. Snodgrass*—A Personal Narrative of the First Anglo-Burmese War 1824 - 1826.

THE HERO OF ALIWAL *by James Humphries*—The Campaigns of Sir Harry Smith in India, 1843-1846, During the Gwalior War & the First Sikh War.

ALL FOR A SHILLING A DAY *by Donald F. Featherstone*—The story of H.M. 16th, the Queen's Lancers During the first Sikh War 1845-1846.

LEONAUR

ALSO FROM LEONAUR
AVAILABLE IN SOFTCOVER OR HARDCOVER WITH DUST JACKET

ZULU:1879 *by D.C.F. Moodie & the Leonaur Editors*—The Anglo-Zulu War of 1879 from contemporary sources: First Hand Accounts, Interviews, Dispatches, Official Documents & Newspaper Reports.

THE RED DRAGOON *by W.J. Adams*—With the 7th Dragoon Guards in the Cape of Good Hope against the Boers & the Kaffir tribes during the 'war of the axe' 1843-48'.

THE RECOLLECTIONS OF SKINNER OF SKINNER'S HORSE *by James Skinner*—James Skinner and his 'Yellow Boys' Irregular cavalry in the wars of India between the British, Mahratta, Rajput, Mogul, Sikh & Pindarree Forces.

A CAVALRY OFFICER DURING THE SEPOY REVOLT *by A. R. D. Mackenzie*—Experiences with the 3rd Bengal Light Cavalry, the Guides and Sikh Irregular Cavalry from the outbreak to Delhi and Lucknow.

A NORFOLK SOLDIER IN THE FIRST SIKH WAR *by J W Baldwin*—Experiences of a private of H.M. 9th Regiment of Foot in the battles for the Punjab, India 1845-6.

TOMMY ATKINS' WAR STORIES: 14 FIRST HAND ACCOUNTS—Fourteen first hand accounts from the ranks of the British Army during Queen Victoria's Empire.

THE WATERLOO LETTERS *by H. T. Siborne*—Accounts of the Battle by British Officers for its Foremost Historian.

NEY: GENERAL OF CAVALRY VOLUME 1—1769-1799 *by Antoine Bulos*—The Early Career of a Marshal of the First Empire.

NEY: MARSHAL OF FRANCE VOLUME 2—1799-1805 *by Antoine Bulos*—The Early Career of a Marshal of the First Empire.

AIDE-DE-CAMP TO NAPOLEON *by Philippe-Paul de Ségur*—For anyone interested in the Napoleonic Wars this book, written by one who was intimate with the strategies and machinations of the Emperor, will be essential reading.

TWILIGHT OF EMPIRE *by Sir Thomas Ussher & Sir George Cockburn*—Two accounts of Napoleon's Journeys in Exile to Elba and St. Helena: Narrative of Events by Sir Thomas Ussher & Napoleon's Last Voyage: Extract of a diary by Sir George Cockburn.

PRIVATE WHEELER *by William Wheeler*—The letters of a soldier of the 51st Light Infantry during the Peninsular War & at Waterloo.

ALSO FROM LEONAUR

AVAILABLE IN SOFTCOVER OR HARDCOVER WITH DUST JACKET

CAPTAIN COIGNET *by Jean-Roch Coignet*—A Soldier of Napoleon's Imperial Guard from the Italian Campaign to Russia and Waterloo.

HUSSAR ROCCA *by Albert Jean Michel de Rocca*—A French cavalry officer's experiences of the Napoleonic Wars and his views on the Peninsular Campaigns against the Spanish, British And Guerilla Armies.

MARINES TO 95TH (RIFLES) *by Thomas Fernyhough*—The military experiences of Robert Fernyough during the Napoleonic Wars.

LIGHT BOB *by Robert Blakeney*—The experiences of a young officer in H.M 28th & 36th regiments of the British Infantry during the Peninsular Campaign of the Napoleonic Wars 1804 - 1814.

WITH WELLINGTON'S LIGHT CAVALRY *by William Tomkinson*—The Experiences of an officer of the 16th Light Dragoons in the Peninsular and Waterloo campaigns of the Napoleonic Wars.

SERGEANT BOURGOGNE *by Adrien Bourgogne*—With Napoleon's Imperial Guard in the Russian Campaign and on the Retreat from Moscow 1812 - 13.

SURTEES OF THE 95TH (RIFLES) *by William Surtees*—A Soldier of the 95th (Rifles) in the Peninsular campaign of the Napoleonic Wars.

SWORDS OF HONOUR *by Henry Newbolt & Stanley L. Wood*—The Careers of Six Outstanding Officers from the Napoleonic Wars, the Wars for India and the American Civil War.

ENSIGN BELL IN THE PENINSULAR WAR *by George Bell*—The Experiences of a young British Soldier of the 34th Regiment 'The Cumberland Gentlemen' in the Napoleonic wars.

HUSSAR IN WINTER *by Alexander Gordon*—A British Cavalry Officer during the retreat to Corunna in the Peninsular campaign of the Napoleonic Wars.

THE COMPLEAT RIFLEMAN HARRIS *by Benjamin Harris as told to and transcribed by Captain Henry Curling, 52nd Regt. of Foot*—The adventures of a soldier of the 95th (Rifles) during the Peninsular Campaign of the Napoleonic Wars.

THE ADVENTURES OF A LIGHT DRAGOON *by George Farmer & G.R. Gleig*—A cavalryman during the Peninsular & Waterloo Campaigns, in captivity & at the siege of Bhurtpore, India.